WALKING THE
WITH MI.

This unique book offers compelling stories to help you encounter life with mindfulness and find new vigor on your teaching path. Author Richard Brady, founder of the Mindfulness in Education Network, shares his experiences in a variety of areas, including motivation, agency and freedom, creativity, nurturing presence and community, and more. Following each story, you'll find reflections and contemplations that invite connection with your own experiences and ultimately with action. The book can be used by educators of all levels and subject areas, for personal use and for in-service and pre-service education.

Richard Brady retired in 2007 after teaching high school mathematics for thirty-seven years. He is a retreat leader, writer, educational consultant, and coordinator of the Wake Up Schools Level II Program in North America. He is a founder of the Mindfulness in Education Network. Visit his website www.mindingourlives.net.

Also Available from Routledge Eye On Education

www.routledge.com/k-12

17 THINGS RESILIENT TEACHERS DO (AND 4 THINGS THEY HARDLY EVER DO)
BRYAN HARRIS

EVERYDAY SEL IN EARLY CHILDHOOD: INTEGRATING SOCIAL-EMOTIONAL LEARNING AND MINDFULNESS INTO YOUR CLASSROOM
CARLA TANTILLO PHILIBERT

EVERYDAY SEL IN ELEMENTARY SCHOOL: INTEGRATING SOCIAL-EMOTIONAL LEARNING AND MINDFULNESS INTO YOUR CLASSROOM
CARLA TANTILLO PHILIBERT

EVERYDAY SEL IN MIDDLE SCHOOL: INTEGRATING SOCIAL-EMOTIONAL LEARNING AND MINDFULNESS INTO YOUR CLASSROOM
CARLA TANTILLO PHILIBERT

EVERYDAY SEL IN HIGH SCHOOL: INTEGRATING SOCIAL-EMOTIONAL LEARNING AND MINDFULNESS INTO YOUR CLASSROOM
CARLA TANTILLO PHILIBERT

EVERYDAY SELF-CARE FOR EDUCATORS: TOOLS AND STRATEGIES FOR WELL-BEING
CARLA TANTILLO PHILIBERT, CHRISTOPHER SOTO, LAURA VEON

MINDFULNESS FOR STUDENTS: A CURRICULUM FOR GRADES 3–8
WENDY WEBER

FIRST AID FOR TEACHER BURNOUT: HOW YOU CAN FIND PEACE AND SUCCESS
JENNY GRANT RANKIN

WALKING THE TEACHER'S PATH WITH MINDFULNESS

Stories for Reflection and Action

Richard Brady

For Amy,

In gratitude for your pioneering role in the mindful education movement.

Many smiles,

Richard

Routledge
Taylor & Francis Group

NEW YORK AND LONDON

First published 2021
by Routledge
605 Third Avenue, New York, NY 10158

and by Routledge
2 Park Square, Milton Park, Abingdon, Oxon, OX14 4RN

Routledge is an imprint of the Taylor & Francis Group, an informa business

Library of Congress Cataloging-in-Publication Data
Names: Brady, Richard (Teacher), author.
Title: Walking the teacher's path with mindfulness : stories for reflection and action / Richard Brady.
Description: New York, NY : Routledge, 2021. | Series: Eye on education
Identifiers: LCCN 2021001533 (print) | LCCN 2021001534 (ebook) | ISBN 9780367741662 (hardback) | ISBN 9780367724535 (paperback) | ISBN 9781003156369 (ebook)
Subjects: LCSH: Teaching–Psychological aspects. | Mindfulness (Psychology)
Classification: LCC LB1027 .B698 2021 (print) | LCC LB1027 (ebook) | DDC 371.102–dc23
LC record available at https://lccn.loc.gov/2021001533
LC ebook record available at https://lccn.loc.gov/2021001534

ISBN: 978-0-367-74166-2 (hbk)
ISBN: 978-0-367-72453-5 (pbk)
ISBN: 978-1-003-15636-9 (ebk)

Typeset in Bembo
by SPi Global, India

CV 06 11 2021 1151

For my teachers and my students

CONTENTS

MEET THE AUTHOR

Richard Brady, MS, retired in 2007 after teaching high school mathematics for thirty-seven years. He is a retreat leader, writer, educational consultant, and coordinator of the Wake Up Schools Level II Program in North America. He is a founder of the Mindfulness in Education Network, an international organization with 1,700 participants. In 2001, he was recognized by Thich Nhat Hanh as a teacher in his tradition with a special focus on cultivating mindfulness in young people. Richard has led retreats and offered workshops for educators in the US, Italy, and Germany. He is an editor of *Tuning In: Mindfulness in Teaching and Learning* (2009). Other writings of his are available at www.mindingourlives.net.

FOREWORD

Progressive educator John Dewey noted that, "We don't learn from experience. We learn from reflecting on experience." Indeed, Richard Brady's book is a meta-reflection on a lifetime of teaching, learning, and living. While Brady has many insights to impart, his chosen medium—the story—is noteworthy. Throughout history, stories have been used to entertain, to teach, to inspire, to kindle empathy, and to reveal life's lessons. More recently, neurological studies reveal that multiple portions of the brain are activated by storytelling—many more than when information is presented didactically. Through a collection of stories and poems, Brady invites readers into a hall of mirrors through which they can reflect on their experiences even as he reflects on his.

As a reader, you are invited along on one person's intellectual and spiritual life journey. However, since the book is organized around a series of universal themes (e.g., Catching fire, Living without boundaries, Interdependence), Brady's stories and poems are transcendent. The reflective questions at the end of each section create a bridge between Brady's experiences and one's own life. They invite readers to reflect on the stories, consider their own circumstances, and derive personal meanings and insights.

As a teacher, you will likely acquire new pedagogical approaches. But you will also gain a new appreciation and empathy for your learners and the context in which deep learning occurs. As a person, you'll be inspired to resurface the stories of your life and to reflect upon and celebrate the insights they enable. And perhaps you'll be inspired to compose your own version of the *Lessons* of your life.

Jay McTighe

A Letter to Readers

Dear Educator,

Why this book? Why now?

These questions are for you as well as me. Please take your time answering them. This project has been sixty years in the making, written now because these challenging times compel me to share some of the lifelong gifts of my lessons in education as teacher and as student.

This book is about change—not that I've always been interested in change. As a young person, if not always happy, I was content with life as it was. My middle-class Jewish family with roots in Germany placed a high value on education, I'd been given a pair of glasses at birth through which I saw and understood the world, but I failed to realize that others might wear glasses with different prescriptions. At sixteen, reading the books of Thomas Wolfe sparked a wonder about life experience other than my own. That spark continued to smolder. I attended MIT and pursued a path to success in a technical field, encouraged by the atmosphere I encountered and an education that extolled life as a professional.

In graduate school at the University of Maryland, I discovered Ken Kesey's *One Flew over the Cuckoo's Nest* and Robert Heinlein's *Stranger in a Strange Land*, both stories in which an outsider attempts to liberate the natives. I also began encountering opportunities for my own short-term liberation—glimpsing certain mysteries during an evening with spiritual teacher Ram Dass and again at a Grateful Dead concert. Eight years after encountering passion in the writing of Thomas Wolfe, I recognized it again reading Henry Miller. Passion, the search for meaning, the search for one's true self—I loved reading about them, even experiencing them briefly, but I never thought of embarking on a path to my own heart. I was conditioned not to change.

In 1970, at age twenty-six, I left my doctoral program in physics and began teaching high school math. Having taken no education courses, I taught in the traditional didactic way I'd learned as a student. That summer after my initial year of teaching a bright first epiphany came to me: I took University of Maryland instructor Ron McKeen's summer school methods course—a joint venture between teacher and students from start to finish. There I was offered a new pair of glasses through which to view teaching, as well as the wider world. I tried them on. Conventional wisdom about teaching and learning ceased to be my standard. From then on and throughout the next fifty years, I would continually develop my own changing theories and practices of education. You will find many of these stories in the following pages, none more important than my discovery, at age forty, of Vietnamese Zen Master Thich Nhat Hanh and the life-changing practice of mindfulness.

We teach what we need to learn. As a husband and father, I was profoundly stimulated to grow, discovering that I needed to learn more about my own agency and about connecting with others. Motivation, independence, connection, and growth—these became focal points of my pedagogy as well. I let intuition guide me in finding teachers, mentors, experiences, and writings that nourished me. Stopping to reflect was important—to assimilate what I'd been learning. But when I stopped too long, something tapped me on the shoulder and whispered, "Time to grow."

For three years I taught at Woodrow Wilson High School in Washington, DC. Wilson was a public school diverse in every respect, a perfect setting for transformation—mine and my students—had I more support. I was a fledgling teacher with large classes and little background in education beyond my own experience as a student. To grow into the educator I hoped to become, I needed to be transplanted. Sidwell Friends, a Quaker school a few blocks away, was akin to New Trier, my own prestigious secondary school in Winnetka, Illinois. I made the move in 1973, ready to cultivate new ways of teaching. And there I also found myself attracted to the calming inner life of Quaker practice.

At the turn of the century, twenty-seven years later, most Sidwell students weren't experiencing social oppression, climate change, or the dwindling resources that affected some, but I could see on the horizon a darker future for all young people. I was already hearing about school shootings, increased pressure on teachers to achieve narrowly measured results, and the effects of video games and social media on young people's attention spans. During 2005–2007, my final years of teaching, I began each math class with five minutes of contemplative practice, helping all of us relax and focus. These were the most rewarding years of my career. However, teaching mindfulness to many students and, especially to teachers, suddenly seemed more compelling than teaching math. Not wanting to be bound by a schoolteacher's schedule, I decided to retire.

Here you will find stories about my mindfulness weekends for educators which I'd already begun to offer and, more recently, five-day and eight-day educators' retreats. In all of these I draw on my life lessons both in and out of the classroom. My thoughts, words, and actions and the ways they've changed over the years have been the result of innumerable causes and conditions— teachers and mentors, books, and, most especially, life experiences. I share only a few in the pages that follow. You and I live in a world of pandemics, social injustice, and climate change, but what you bring to teaching is unique to you. These stories are not intended as a model or prescription. However you receive them, may they prompt you to engage with the queries that follow them as a way of reflecting on your own life lessons.

Regarding the two questions that open this letter: Why this book? Why now? If you've arrived at this point, you have your answers. You are ready to proceed. Go slowly and enjoy your journey.

Richard Brady
Putney, Vermont, USA

ACKNOWLEDGEMENTS

It took a village to raise this teacher and this book:

This Teacher

Family—my beloved partner and faithful editor Elisabeth whose life embodies growth, my brother Bob, whose life was the source of my inspiration to be an educator, my parents Jane and Rudy, my children and their partners Shoshanna and Nick, Patrick and Hanick, and grandchildren Jane Maple, Yakiyn, Zuriel, Kadmiel, and Carna whose love nurtures me on my journey.

Teachers and Mentors—Thich Nhat Hanh, whose teaching helps me live a life of understanding and service; Parker Palmer, who introduced me to teaching from the heart; Bob Burton, whose understanding of people and the world was an ongoing support for my life and my teaching; David Mallery, my first seat cheerleader and model connector; Rev. Paula Wehmiller, for her listening and wisdom; Earl Harrison, for his friendship and heartful leadership; Ron McKeen, with whom students became teachers; Jim Landers, who introduced me to myself; Sid Parnes, my creativity guide; fellow Deadhead and mindful therapist Ted Cmarada; and Neil Davidson, who introduced me to small-group and discovery learning.

Co-facilitators—Irene McHenry, for co-leading numerous mindfulness retreats for educators and co-editing one collection of mindfulness stories for them; Susan Murphy, with whom I took the leap to lead educator retreats; Beth Popelka, friend and co-instigator of "Minding Our Lives" weekends: Letizia and Stefano Carboni, Marco Spirandelli, Beppe Gambardella and the rest of the moveable Avalokita staff, for their love and their support; Sr. Annabel and Sr. Jewel, who first invited me to co-lead an educator retreat in Germany in Thich Nhat Hanh's tradition; Valerie Brown, John Bell, Elli Weisbaum, Fern Dorresteyn, and the monastics at Blue Cliff and Magnolia Grove Monasteries, with whom I shared this same privilege in the US; and long before these events Joan Countryman and Arthur Powell, for inviting me to join them in leading "Creative Approaches to Secondary School Mathematics;" and Linda Munger, for coming on board at the last minute to co-lead "Exploring Staff Development Together."

Programs and Schools—I owe so much to my friend and colleague Jay McTighe for creating St. Mary's Center for Interdisciplinary Studies, where all my creative juices were drawn forth, and the amazing staff Jay gathered together summer after summer; to the Sidwell Friends Upper School mathematics faculty, who humored me over years of experimentation; Ellen Pierson, my friend and go-to support person; Neal Tonken, my writing coach; and to my many other Sidwell Friends colleagues over the years.

Mindfulness Education Colleagues—Br. Phap Luu and Orla O'Sullivan, guiding lights for Thich Nhat Hanh's "Wake Up Schools" initiative and Katherine Weare, friend, colleague, and co-author with Thich Nhat Hanh of *Happy Teachers Change the World*; and my many companions on the Mindfulness in Education Network's Board, especially MiEN's Presidents Katie Byrnes, Chris Willard, and Elizabeth Kriynovich.

The Village of Students—ever-changing, ever with me, as I walked the teacher's path.

This Book

Editorial help—As a first-time author, I have tremendous gratitude to Lauren Davis, my editor at Routledge, who was available virtually 24/7 to answer questions and give advice and my friend Matt Friberg at Routledge, who tutored me in publishing. As I was writing this manuscript and the memoir which birthed it, old friend, poet, and editor Judith Toy schooled me in writing as she went over my manuscripts, breathing life into my words. Garrett Phelan, another old friend, poet, and writing teacher, also read my manuscripts and let me know from the start that the memoir was really two or three different books. However, I clung to it until Parallax Press editor Hisae Matsuda told me the same thing. Terry Barber, friend and publishing liaison. My too soon departed sister in mindfulness and writing, Susan Hadler, read my manuscripts, cheered me on, and inspired me with her own commitment to writing. Other friends who weighed in on my manuscripts included educator/writer/pediatrician Dzung Vo, transformative educator and writer Diego James Navarro, writer and editor Gene Klinger, perceptive connector Linnie Jones, Quaker visionary and writer Noah Merrill, and poet and writing teacher Kate Gleason.

Friends who gave valued feedback on sections of the book include Arnie Kotler, founder of Parallax Press; Nonviolent Communication Trainer Peggy Smith; former Plum Village monastic Barbara Newell; Amy Saltzman, founder of the Association for Mindfulness in Education; and mindfulness in education writer Lauren Alderfer.

Friends Teresa Savel, Steve Marcus, Jesse Palidofsky, Coni Richards, and Nathalie Martin, who gave me their moral support throughout the writing and publishing. And, my friend Börje Tobiasson, whose powerful photo graces the cover of this book.

INTRODUCTION

I discovered stories as a teaching tool in 1984 when I was a student of educator, author, and activist Parker Palmer at Pendle Hill Quaker Center in Wallingford, Pennsylvania. Every week Parker gave our class stories from the Taoist tradition to read, contemplate, and journal on. From these I went on to encounter many stories from other wisdom traditions, buying books of stories, hearing stories in talks I attended, and coming upon stories as authors used them to make points. I remember stories long after I've forgotten discursive accounts. Some of the most powerful stories I've ever read are from Dr. Rachel Naomi Remen's book *Kitchen Table Wisdom: Stories that Heal*[1]—stories about Dr. Remen's patients, her interactions with other physicians, and her own healing. Knowing first-hand how little time educators have to read for their own edification, sharing my experiences in the form of stories seemed fitting. I love to tell stories as well as read them.

I've benefited from many exceptional teachers and mentors. I hope my experiences inspire other educators. But can stories offer educators something more than inspiration? Can reading stories about education benefit their work? In my experience, if the readers are given the opportunity to make their own meaning, a story is more likely to connect to their lives and remain alive and at work in their consciousness. To that end, distinguished educator Diego James Navarro suggested I include queries following each story for readers to reflect on. We've both benefited from contemplating and reflecting on queries in Quaker contexts, mining readings and talks for deeper relevance. "Contemplate a meaningful experience you had as a new teacher. What did you learn from it about teaching? About yourself?" These questions ask readers first to dwell with an experience, then reflect on it. Reading a story and contemplating or reflecting on queries can happen before turning out the light at night, as a prelude to journaling, or in a group of educators where reflections are shared. Reflection and contemplation differ. The former is intellectual in nature, involving thought; the latter is meditative, a dwelling with. The queries in this book are referred to as "Reflections and Contemplations." Some may set you to thinking straightaway. Others may invite you into a space of images and feelings, a space of pure experience, a contemplative space. A contemplation may give way to reflection. Or vice versa.

Reflection and contemplation are forms of action. Whether or not you begin to make changes in your teaching, read other books, or simply share your thoughts with others, reflection and contemplation change you in subtle ways that can lead to these and other actions in the future. Many of the stories in this book describe my actions as an educator. For most of my career I was fortunate to teach in settings where change was possible and even supported. However, I feel that the most significant action I took was as a first year teacher in a large, urban, public high school, where I proposed to my principal that I create and teach a course for students who were not interested in continuing their study of mathematics.

In addition to wanting my stories to connect with you, the reader, I've connected them with other stories related to one of four themes: *Catching Fire, Living Without Boundaries, Seeing With the Heart*, and *Walking My Path*. These themes aren't peculiar to education. They're the stuff of life itself! Additionally, there are themes that appear again and again throughout the book: collaboration, creativity, joy, and transformation. The talks I give also have themes and include stories. In both cases, cohesion, not chronology is my guide. However, the order of the stories is important. Later stories refer to and add dimension to earlier ones, so you may find it helpful to read the stories in the order they appear. I encourage you, however, to periodically revisit stories to mine them for new meaning and new connections with your own experience.

In the Parts that follow, you will find stories that address:

Part I: Catching Fire—motivating individuals, classes, and parents; forms of motivation; acceptance as motivator; exemplary motivators; the power of volition

Part II: Living Without Boundaries—nurturing autonomy; outer freedom and inner freedom; creativity; transcending separation in school and in life; accepting uncertainty; taking risks

Part III: Seeing With the Heart—stopping; beholding life with wonder; being with others and oneself; creating spaces for deep connection; responding from a place of freedom

Part IV: Walking My Path—skillful means; happiness; suffering and transformation; living our truth; celebrating life

This book is not written to give advice on how or what to teach. Parker Palmer tells us, "We teach who we are."[2] Each of us is unique and "who we are" ever-changing. I hope my stories illuminate for you some of the myriad factors that influence change and growth—that of teachers, of students, of everyone. Whether or not you're an educator, may these stories help you see your work and your life with new eyes.

NOTES

1 Remen, R. N. (1996). *Kitchen table wisdom: Stories that heal.* New York: Riverhead Books.

2 Palmer, P. (2017). *The courage to teach: Exploring the inner landscape of a teacher's life.* San Francisco, CA: Jossey-Bass.

PART I

CATCHING FIRE

Don't ask what the world needs. Ask what makes you come alive and go out and do it. Because what the world needs is people who have come alive.

—Howard Thurman[1]

Catching fire—motivation—is complex and mysterious. What I've learned about it has come from reflecting on my own learning experience, those of my students, experiences with teaching—my own and others', and wisdom shared directly with me and drawn from books. Fires begin to burn only when conditions are sufficient, and countless ingredients contribute to the fuel. In the following stories these include particular teachers, situations, environments, activities, groups, books, and challenges. The fuel mixture must be appropriate for the learner and the learner must be primed for ignition for combustion to occur. An old maxim suggests that, "When the learner is ready, the teacher will appear." But even when the fire kindled is but a small one or dies out when conditions change, embers can remain and reignite years later.

What makes our students come alive? In 1980 I'd been teaching high school math at Sidwell Friends School in Washington, DC for seven years when I was presented with an unusual opportunity to examine this question. Almon was a sophomore. He wasn't a student of mine, but I'd been having conversations with him since he brought his box of childhood toys to school and placed it in the hall in front of his locker.

One day Almon bemoaned his current experience with mathematics:

"Before last year I attended St. Albans and never enjoyed math. Last year I lived in Boston and attended Commonwealth School. My math teacher there got me really excited about math. Now I've come to Sidwell, and I no longer enjoy it."

"Almon," I replied, "were you excited about math at Commonwealth or were you excited about your teacher? If it was math you were excited about, my guess is you'd still be excited about it this year regardless of the teacher."

Almon was skeptical.

John Holt, author of *How Children Fail*[2] and one of my education heroes, had taught at Commonwealth, which held up one rule: *No roller skating in the halls. In other words, Don't be a damn fool.* I'd always wanted to visit there. I asked Almon the name of his teacher. On our next professional development day I paid a visit to Commonwealth. Just as I suspected—Almon's teacher projected his exuberance about math and kept his class on the edge of their seats with his inspired rhetoric and well-timed questions. Here at the front of the class was the charismatic teacher I was not.

As a student, I never experienced a teacher like Almon's. I had excellent high school math teachers, but my total engagement in their classes was primarily motivated by my own interest in math, supported by their clear explanations and the challenging assigned and extra credit problems they gave us. English was a different story.

I grew up with little interest in literature or writing. Raised in a family where emotional expression wasn't the *lingua franca*, my understanding of books and my self-expression were limited. Fortunately, in eleventh grade reading opened a door, exposing me to a vast range of emotions and to families that didn't look like mine. I discovered new dimensions of life. My soft-spoken English teacher, Mr. Landers, helped me investigate American literature in a fresh way, to connect it with my own experience. Junior year at Winnetka, Illinois' New Trier High School included writing the dreaded *Junior Theme*, an analysis of the works of an author selected by the student. Leaning on Mr. Landers' advice, I choose Thomas Wolfe. *Thomas Wolfe: A Theme* was the most important paper I wrote in all my school years. In Eugene Gant, the protagonist of Wolfe's first novel *Look Homeward Angel*,[3] I found a character who spoke for me. For the first time, I found myself intensely interested in developing and communicating my own thoughts. My feeling of self-worth increased in response to Mr. Landers' encouragement and approval and infused my writing. I was exploring myself.

With Mr. Landers' urging I moved up to honors English for senior year. In Mr. Boyle's world literature class, my classmates were mostly members of New Trier's literary and arts set, well versed in literary analysis and writing. None of us were prepared for Mr. Boyle. The year started with impossible, out-of-the-blue spelling and abbreviation tests. Were they, like the slap of a Zen master, intended to humble the better students? I had no idea, but I was more curious than anxious. In contrast to Mr. Landers, Mr. Boyle was far more critical of my work. Did I know how to read? I soon discovered that I didn't know how to delve beneath the surface. Focusing my latent analytical skills on my own ideas was slow going, but my experience with Mr. Landers gave me confidence in their worth. Without that, I'm not sure I would have mustered the strength to survive Mr. Boyle's critiques.

For the fall semester Mr. Boyle gave me a 'C', my worst grade in all of high school. Grades were important to my parents. Making a fuss about our success, they rewarded my brother and me for good report cards. They didn't ask about my grade in Mr. Boyle's class. They assumed I did not and could not deserve a 'C'.

"Mr. Boyle is probably prejudiced. You should ask for a transfer," my mother said, trying to minimize the suffering she assumed I felt.

I was angry, a rare state. For me, the 'C' had a different significance. I knew I deserved it. I still had a lot to learn from Mr. Boyle. With a fresh sense of personal power, I asked my parents to stay out of it.

During the second semester, I wrote a five-page paper for Mr. Boyle on "Petition,"[4] W.H. Auden's 100-word poem beseeching God to intervene in a world gone awry. Removed though I felt from a higher power, I was drawn to the idea of prayer as an avenue of radical change. I also wrote a paper upholding the Athenian jurors' verdict of Socrates as guilty. Putting myself in the jurors' shoes, I argued that Socrates, through teaching the youth, threatened society. I got so involved in writing my opus that there was no way I could finish it on time. Since the paper was already late, I decided to take the time to thoroughly complete it. Writing a paper that I wanted to write was a new experience. I loved it!

At the end of second semester, I received an 'A' from Mr. Boyle—satisfying but unneeded. I already felt grateful. Reading and writing had begun to come alive for me. I was developing an understanding of literature, complementing the new understanding of myself developed in Mr. Landers' English class the previous year. Both of these jewels I carried tenderly as I continued on my path. My newfound interest in literature became a part of me.

REFLECTIONS AND CONTEMPLATIONS

As the Thurman quote advises, ask what makes you come alive.

Visualize a time when you came alive.

What ingredients—people, place, situation, feelings, hopes—helped make this possible?

When have you seen one of your students come alive?

What conditions helped promote this?

STUDENT-LED LEARNING

Sometimes the teacher and the subject matter prove insufficient to kindle a fire. In the early 1990s an afternoon ninth/tenth grade algebra class was giving me fits. The students didn't seem to be able to settle down. They finished only half the work my morning group completed. This was very unusual for Sidwell, where students placed a high value on success. My first impulse was to blame their difficulties on a clique of immature ninth-graders.

I wasn't hesitant to ask friends for advice about personal problems. However, I was an experienced teacher. I should not have been having difficulty handling a class. I should know what to do. I was too proud to ask a colleague for help. By December I was at my wits' end. When an opportunity for assistance presented itself, I reached out gratefully for help for the first time. I shared my problem with Marci, a visiting educational consultant.

Marci asked whether I was sure of my suspicions about the immature students.

"I'm not," I answered.

"Why don't you ask the class what the problem is?"

"I never thought of doing that," I replied.

I conducted an anonymous survey. The results were surprising. Students responded that they were tired because the class met right after lunch. Reporting this "finding" to the class, I told them I'd do some research over winter break and see if I could find a remedy.

I spent part of my break at a small meditation center in nearby West Virginia. Rahula, one of the teachers there, was a yoga practitioner. When I asked his advice, Rahula told me about *qi* (a Chinese word pronounced "chi," meaning life force energy) and showed me an exercise that brings *qi* up from the feet.

Stand on your toes with your hands over your head. Breathe out as you bend down and touch the floor. Then breathe in and slowly straighten, raising your hands back up over your head. Repeat this exercise nine more times, remaining on your toes.

With Rahula's remedy, I returned to my challenging after-lunch class. Gathering the students in a circle, I led them in the exercise. We all reported feeling invigorated. The lesson that followed went well. "In the future," I told them, "we'll start each class this way. I'll ask you to take turns leading it. If you're wide awake and ready for class, participation will be optional." For the remainder of the year almost all of us joined in this daily exercise. People passing our door peered in its window with surprise. Our opening practice came to be our novel class signature. Best of all, students became more focused on work and more attentive both to me and to one another. This was not my last experience of looking to students for direction.

I'd been released from teaching mathematics at Sidwell Friends for the 2000–2001 school year to teach mindfulness off campus. During that year I offered two educator workshops and visited schools, presenting assemblies on mindfulness and faculty workshops. A Friends school I visited invited me to meet first with faculty members interested in mindfulness at the end of the school day and then return the following day to teach mindfulness to some of their classes.

Most of the teachers gave me some idea of what I might share with their students. But I had no clue as to the approach to take with a ninth grade English class studying *Catcher in the Rye*.[5] I'd never read the book, and I'd never walked into a classroom, much less a room of unfamiliar students, without some idea of the lesson. I introduced myself, telling the students I taught high school math and meditation as well. Then I asked, "Why do you think your teacher invited me to teach you meditation?" A number of hands shot up. I took notes as students responded and let them guide me in shaping what followed.

One student suggested I might have been invited to help them meditate on Holden Caulfield's life, another because this class tended to be restless. "It must have been the latter," I told them, and followed this fortuitous opening with a relaxation practice from Vietnamese Zen master Thich Nhat Hanh, asking the students to focus on their breath as I led them:

> Breathing in, I know I am breathing in.
> Breathing out, I know I am breathing out.
> Breathing in, my breath grows deep.
> Breathing out, my breath grows slow.
> Breathing in, I feel calm.
> Breathing out, I feel ease.
> Breathing in, I smile.
> Breathing out, I release.
> Dwelling in the present moment,
> I know it is a wonderful moment.[6]

Motivating a class is usually the province of subject matter and teacher. But this isn't always the case. Student-led learning sprouts from the students themselves, aided by skillful gardening from teachers. This was true of the stretching practice that arose in response to the tiredness identified by my algebra students and this relaxation meditation which addressed what a student identified as "class restlessness."

REFLECTIONS AND CONTEMPLATIONS

Have you experienced student-led learning in the classroom as a teacher? As a student? If so, what were the circumstances?

Contemplate a time when someone asked you, "Are you sure?"

When you asked yourself, "Am I sure?"

Where did these experiences lead?

ACCEPTANCE AND SELF-ACCEPTANCE

Acceptance provides students and teachers rich soil for growth. When we enter a classroom, each of us arrives with our own thoughts and feelings. Opening activities that welcome these differences communicate recognition and caring for us as whole people. This goes hand in hand with an absence of judgment and can entail an element of choice. Additionally, experiences of acceptance by others promote self-acceptance.

During my last two years of teaching at Sidwell Friends I began every math class with five minutes of mindfulness practice.[7] My favorite was journal writing. I gave students journals the first day of class and kept them stored in the closet of my classroom until the end of the year. Some days, after a period of contemplation, I invited the class to write about a challenging problem or question in their journals or about some aspect of the course. They wrote these entries in the front of the journals. I read them at the end of the week and wrote, "Thank you. RB." Appreciation was the most supportive response I could give. Most Fridays we practiced free writing. The students and I wrote continuously for five minutes, putting down on paper whatever was in our minds. Other writing days we responded to prompts such as short stories from wisdom traditions, poems, or one of several quotations that approached a common theme from different angles. Students did the latter writing in the back of their journals with the understanding that I wouldn't read them.

When students got tired of the kinds of prompts I gave them, I'd find new sources. One day in my tenth-grade honors geometry course I surprised students by telling them they'd receive a quote from Malcolm X to reflect on the following day. Here it is:

> I'm sorry to say that the subject I most disliked was mathematics. I have thought about it. I think the reason was that mathematics leaves no room for argument. If you made a mistake, that was all there was to it.[8]

Their responses to this quote were written in the back of their journals, so, by agreement, I didn't read them. I wish I'd been able to, as the quote suggests why inviting contemplation in the learning process was challenging. The students had grown up with the understanding that math problems had one right answer and their job was to find it. From the moment they encountered a problem, they began analyzing it, comparing it to problems they'd already solved, seeing what known properties might be relevant, and so on. Sitting back and simply contemplating a figure or a question, waiting patiently for insight to arrive rarely happened.

Journal writing engaged almost all the students because I gave them an invitation to write whatever they thought about. There were no wrong responses and no critiques, even when their responses were for me. Students could lambast the prompts I gave them or wander far from them in their thinking and writing. Only once did a student object to free writing. He was an artist and didn't enjoy writing. Could he draw? Sure, if he continuously rendered visually whatever entered his mind. There was the question of what he would draw when his mind was empty. When other students encountered this, I asked that they write, "My mind is blank" over and over until something showed up. This issue never confronted the artist.

Although I never read the entries in the backs of student journals, I was curious about them. Towards the end of the year I asked all students to read all their own back-of-the-journal entries and write a paper describing one of these entries and why it was meaningful. A number picked free writing entries written early in the year and commented on how much their attitudes about the course or their understanding of mathematics had changed. One wrote:

What I have learned is that dealing with adversity and solving difficult problems is as much about the way you think about thinking about the problem as it is the problem itself. If you allow yourself to forget about the intimidation, to forget about your preconceived notions about what you are doing; if you get into a focused, creative mindset, and immerse yourself in the situation, then and only then can you reach your full potential.

In the end, students always made their own meanings. In responding to readings, one wrote, she would often "stray away from it (the reading) to my own thoughts." Another went further:

I have learned great things from myself in the way that I respond to quotes in my journal and in how I respond to myself in free writing. In writing continuously, I often write things that I did not understand consciously before they hit the paper.

Lectio Divina, or divine reading (Latin), is a monastic practice dating back to the sixth century. In essence, it involves dwelling with a short scriptural passage, taking it in without analysis. This contemplative mode of learning is quite different from those found in most schools. I employ *Lectio Divina* in mindfulness workshops for educators, to offer them the opportunity to connect deeply with a poem or short text.

In preparing a workshop for the opening faculty meeting of an independent high school, I located this practice toward the end. I hoped that sharing in pairs after contemplative reading and journaling would deepen faculty connections and help the workshop conclude on a dynamic note. A new school year was about to commence. I used "beginnings" as a common theme for the passages faculty members chose from. I selected a fanciful story about beginnings from my collection of tales and added three quotes I found by searching "beginnings; quotations" on Google. The four passages, each with a different perspective on beginning follow. The energy of the pair sharing that followed revealed the dynamic connections the teachers had made with their chosen quotes.

What we call the beginning is often the end. And to make an end is to make a beginning. The end is where we start from.

T.S. Eliot[9]

Young Nasrudin decided to learn an instrument, so he called upon a music instructor.

"How much do you charge for private lute lessons?" asked the boy.

"The lute is not an easy instrument to learn," answered the teacher. "I charge three silver coins for the first month, and one silver piece for each month after that."

"Fine," agreed Nasrudin. "I'll start with the second month."

Sufi[10]

The only trust required is to know that when there is one ending there will be another beginning.

Clarissa Pinkola Estés[11]

All this will not be finished in the first 100 days. Nor will it be finished in the first 1,000 days, not in the life of this Administration, nor even perhaps in our lifetime on this planet. But let us begin.

John Fitzgerald Kennedy[12]

Following the workshop, a first-year teacher thanked me and told me, "I'd like to start my teaching here with the second year." The tale had done its job.

Providing students and educators with choices to participate in yoga or not, to draw rather than write, to contemplate a particular passage that spoke to them set a tone of invitation that was continually welcomed.

Self-acceptance is a key ingredient of motivation. Some students seem always to bounce back from difficulties. Others get lost. It's as though their mind tells them they're incapable. Quizzes, tests, and exams were major sources of stress for many students. Some came to class so stressed that their ability to show what they knew was compromised. My setting aside five minutes for meditation before the start of quizzes, tests, and exams proved to be very beneficial for many of them. I started this practice before the first quiz by asking the class if anyone felt nervous. When hands went up, I told the class we'd do a short meditation aimed at preparing them to do their best.

The meditation was in two parts. I asked the students to sit, close their eyes, and keep their bodies erect but relaxed. In the first part of the meditation, students turned their attention to their feelings, noticing any nervousness, excitement, or worry, and simply let it be there. Experiencing these emotions is natural. While some emotions aren't helpful, there's nothing intrinsically wrong with them. I suggested to the students that learning to accept these emotions as natural parts of ourselves helps all of us avoid magnifying their effects.

On the other hand, there was more to students' experience of mathematics than this quiz and these feelings. Next I instructed students to change their focus and tune into a time when they had a very positive experience with math. This may have been a recent course, project, or activity or perhaps a memory from long ago of learning to count or tell time. Sitting with feelings of accomplishment for a couple of minutes readied most students to begin the quiz with a positive mindset. I further suggested that if students found themselves getting nervous as they worked, they could stop, close their eyes, breathe in and out slowly three times, and get back in touch with their positive experience.

Here's an end-of-the-year observation from a 10th grade student:

> During the course of this year the meditations at the beginning of class and before tests and quizzes have really taught me to relax. At the beginning of the year I would get nervous before tests and quizzes because I would quickly try to review everything we needed to know, but for the second half of the year, I learned to clear my head. More importantly, I learned to breathe! I learned how to clear my mind and trust that I would remember all of the theorems and formulas. When I was able to clear my head and relax, I made fewer and fewer mistakes.

A few students, like this one, told me it wouldn't help them to meditate beforehand. Could they use the time to study instead? It wouldn't be fair if they were reviewing notes while others weren't,

I said, but it would be fine for them to use the time to think over what they'd been studying. As this student suggests, these students soon chose to meditate.

REFLECTIONS AND CONTEMPLATIONS

Recall a time when you felt accepted by others.

What conditions contributed to this, e.g. openness, vulnerability, deep listening?

What factors contribute to your own self-acceptance? What make it difficult?

Lay aside this book. Take out a pen, a journal or piece of paper and write continuously for five minutes. Put down on paper whatever is in your mind.

What did you notice in doing this?

WHAT THEY'RE INTERESTED IN

In 2001 I began teaching a single 45-minute class on stress reduction as part of the health unit in Freshman Studies, an ungraded one-semester course required of all ninth graders. I based my class on mindfulness. Although Sidwell Friends was a high-stress environment for many, I suspected it wouldn't be easy to engage groups of 13- and 14-year-olds. In his book *Teacher Man*,[13] author Frank McCourt wrote about connecting with his unmotivated New York City high school English class. "What is it they're interested in?" he asked himself. The answers were immediate: sex and food. He introduced a hugely successful unit in which students collected and recited family recipes, some with musical accompaniment provided by classmates. My classes wouldn't be as challenging as McCourt's. However, asking kids to attend fully to anything with nonjudgmental awareness and an attitude of curiosity was asking them to care. Extending care requires a vulnerability some resist. To care involves taking a risk in the face of possible scoffing and ridicule in the ever-judgmental peer atmosphere. I carefully selected what I asked my students to focus on, considering McCourt's question "What interests them?" At their age young people were figuring out who they were. They had great interest in themselves, their peers, and their bodies. For these students, the mind was a fresh frontier. Inviting them to observe their mental activity when their minds were "at rest" became the basis of my exercise, "Mind as a Stage."

I began the lesson by suggesting that our minds play a significant role in our well-being:

> When I talk about *mind*, I'm talking about awareness. It will help to think of your awareness as a 'stage.' On your stage

a succession of actors will make their appearance: thoughts, feelings, perceptions, physical sensations.

Once we were comfortable in our seats, we conducted a short experiment—observing our personal stages. I asked students to close their eyes and tune in to whatever might appear on their stage. "Just watch. Whatever thoughts, feelings, perceptions, or sensations arise during the next few minutes, continue observing. Don't get carried away by anything you see."

After five minutes, the students slowly opened their eyes. The room felt gathered in silence. Keeping students involved, I quietly posed a series of questions about their experience. How many were aware of physical sensations—sounds ... smells ... tastes ... contact with their seat ... heartbeat ... breathing ... feet ... other body parts? How many were aware of emotions? Thoughts? Who saw a thought arise? A thought end? Who experienced negative thoughts or feelings? Many acknowledged having negative thoughts or feelings evoked by events that had already happened or by anticipated future events, a few by the present.

I pointed out that what our minds do during any particular five-minute interval of our waking life is repeated approximately seventy thousand times each year. If we multiplied the number of negative thoughts and emotions we observed by 70,000, we could appreciate why the mind played such a significant role in creating stress and tension. If we were aware of the negative thoughts and feelings that fill our minds and if we could develop ways to replace them with positive thoughts and feelings, we could live happier, less anxious lives in and out of school. As we would soon see, I told them, meditation is one means of helping our minds turn to wholesome thoughts.

"The mind is like a cable television set (a form of media popular with teens at the time)," I explained to the students.

It has many channels, including the happiness, the boredom, the confidence, and the anxiety channels. All people have the same channels, but their reception strengths vary. The strongest ones are default channels, ones that tune in automatically much of the time. If these are negative channels, it's like watching a stressful show over and over. Chronic stress can be the eventual result.

Then I offered one way to change the channel, leading the students in the following guided meditation from Thich Nhat Hanh to tune their awareness to several positive channels: solidity, freshness, and freedom. In the future, when students found their minds fixed on negative channels, they could use this mindfulness exercise to prevent stress from building up. In fact, if they developed a meditation practice and tuned to positive channels regularly, in time these positive channels might become their default channels.

> Breathing in, I know I am breathing in.
> Breathing out, I know I am breathing out.
> Breathing in, I see myself as a flower.
> Breathing out, I feel fresh.
> Breathing in, I see myself as a mountain.
> Breathing out, I feel solid.
> Breathing in, I see myself as still water.
> Breathing out, I reflect all that is.
> Breathing in, I see myself as space.
> Breathing out, I feel free.[14]

Frank McCourt's question, "What is it they're interested in?" also inspired my math teaching. I was concerned that my students had no choice about the mathematics they studied and little idea of where it came from. Some found math interesting. Many were more interested in doing well. I came up with the idea of giving students an opportunity to write a short report on a mathematician of their choice, a project not for a grade or for me, but for themselves.

Sidwell Friends students weren't necessarily interested in the careers of mathematicians, but they were interested in their own careers. I invited students to write letters applying for summer internships with famous mathematicians. The students were to reflect on their own interests and investigate mathematicians who inspired them. Their letters were to communicate both gratitude for the mathematician's contributions and specific reasons why the students felt drawn to the mathematicians' body of work. Many students were charged with new energy.

McCourt's question also proved helpful to me in a situation involving disruptive student behavior. Two friends in one of my classes, both good athletes, had gotten in the habit of kicking and tripping each other like a couple of puppies. Discipline was rarely a problem at Sidwell. I was caught off guard and wary of disturbing the positive spirit of the class. Since I'd been sharing mindfulness practice with my math students, I wondered if there was a way to employ it in this situation. Humbled to reach out for help, I posted a description of my challenge on the Mindfulness in Education Network's[15] listserv. Seventy-eight educators initiated this listserv in 2001 following two mindfulness retreats with Vietnamese Zen master, writer, and peace activist Thich Nhat Hanh. Over the intervening years it had grown considerably. It regularly featured thoughtful discussions, so I knew I'd receive good advice. Of four supportive replies, the one related to the Japanese martial art of aikido was ideal for these athletes. I met with the young men individually and described the principles of aikido. "When your attacker comes at you, you gracefully stand aside and turn his energy back on him rather than oppose him and give away your power," I explained. Each boy understood right away and agreed not to respond to his friend's provocations if his friend also agreed. The three of us then met and sealed the agreement. There were no further incidents.

Teachers have an easier time starting fires under younger students, but meeting their interests still helps. For Mary Scattergood, a second-grade teacher at Friends School Haverford, the answer to McCourt's question was Beanie Babies. After her effort to help her students quiet themselves by meditating on their breath failed to hold their attention, Scattergood asked her students to bring their Beanie Babies to class. The following day, her charges lay prone, treasured animals on their bellies. Beanie Babies rose on each inbreath and fell on each outbreath. "The room was magically still," she reported.[16]

REFLECTIONS AND CONTEMPLATIONS

Recall a time when you felt stressed and how you responded to it.

How have you supported stressed students?

Recall a time when you were invited to explore an interest of your own.

When have you invited a student to follow up on an interest he or she had?

FOOD

While Frank McCourt's successful use of food to motivate students seemed relatively straightforward, including food in my own teaching brought some unexpected results. One occurred when my daughter Shoshanna's fifth-grade class was studying Asian religions. She volunteered me to come to her school and teach her class meditation. Cookie-eating meditation was an obvious approach. At my request, the teacher baked chocolate chip cookies.

To begin class, I told the children that the Buddha lived in India 2,600 years ago. His name, given him by his followers, means "the one who is awake." He'd gotten this name because he'd learned to live deeply in the present moment and not lose himself in thoughts about the past or the future. Meditation was the main method the Buddha and his students used to develop this kind of awareness. It involves keeping your attention on one thing. I told the class we would be giving our attention to eating two cookies. I asked the children whether they thought they could give their full attention to tasting, chewing, and swallowing the cookies very slowly. They smiled and told me they could.

As I was eating my first cookie, I looked up to see how the students were doing. They all appeared completely engaged. I noticed, however, that the class teacher hadn't begun to eat hers. She was looking around the room. As I picked up my second cookie, I noticed the teacher still hadn't begun to eat her first. She kept looking in the direction of Billy, a boy whose hyperactivity was legendary. I spoke quietly to the teacher, assuring her that everything was fine and that she could eat her cookies. The teacher and all the students but one finished eating both cookies after five minutes. That student was Billy, still deeply engrossed in finishing his first. I was thrilled he'd been able to focus his attention on eating and wondered if the teacher had been able to also.

I found a natural place for eating meditation in my math classes at Sidwell. Students would often ask if they could have a party during the last class before a vacation. After I began to practice mindfulness, I saw this as an opportunity for students to experience mindful eating. "Yes and we can eat during our party tomorrow," I'd say, "but it will be a special kind of eating." The following day the students would eat cookies and sip apple cider attentively. Afterwards, they shared their experiences with much gratitude. Several years after I'd begun hosting these parties, I received a memorable response. After all the other students had left the classroom, a 16-year-old girl stopped by my desk to thank me. "I want to tell you, Mr. Brady, that I've had a problem with food. This experience has given me a new, healthier way to relate to it." I was moved and grateful.

Eating meditation has also been an important component of my work with older students and educators, though not always appreciated. In these settings I use raisins rather than cookies. Twice my friend Peter invited me to lead mindfulness workshops for his fourth-year students in the UMass School of Nursing. My own recent surgery prior to the second workshop reminded me of the importance of nurses focusing on their work, particularly on their patients. To practice fully attending to a single activity, I gave the student nurses three raisins. I then instructed them on how to eat mindfully:

> Pick up one raisin and examine it closely. Feel its texture. Squeeze it. Smell it. Put it in your mouth and feel its texture with your tongue. Bite into it. Taste the flavor. Chew it slowly, moving it around in your mouth. Notice how the flavor and texture change. Continue chewing it until all trace of the raisin has vanished from your mouth. Then repeat this with the next raisin. You'll have five minutes for this exercise. The object is not to finish all three raisins but to really eat however many you do get to.

As I was about to sound the bell signaling the start of eating meditation, I saw a student frowning. I was reminded that not everyone enjoys raisins. "Oh, I forgot to ask. Do some of you dislike raisins?" Several hands went up, including the frowner's. "This exercise will be especially challenging for those of you who don't like raisins. It will be easy for your prejudices and memories of previous experiences with raisins to intrude on your mind, making it difficult to give your full awareness to your current experience. If you're able to stay focused on the raisin in your mouth, you stand to gain much more from this exercise than others who enjoy eating raisins."

After five minutes of silent eating, I asked for comments and questions. One student related that she had really enjoyed the exercise but would never have time to eat this way in normal life. Others nodded in agreement. Then the frowner raised her hand. "I really don't like raisins at all," she said, "so I ate each raisin as quickly as I could in order to be through with them." "Unfortunately," I told her, "that approach won't be effective when you become a nurse and some of your patients are raisins." While my bit of humor didn't seem to register with this student, I hoped some of her classmates would take with them the appreciation that nurses practice mindfulness to benefit not only themselves but also their patients.

REFLECTIONS AND CONTEMPLATIONS

Recall a time when you experienced something familiar as if for the first time.

What did you discover? What surprised you?

How can this experience be relevant to your teaching?

Recall a time in your life when, like my student with food issues, seeing with new eyes changed your relationship to a personal challenge.

PARENTS

After teaching Sidwell Friends ninth graders about stress reduction for several years, a parent group invited me to offer a mindfulness workshop for parents. For two years I offered them stress reduction workshops similar to those I gave their students. The turnout was disappointing. When asked to continue a third year, I stopped to reflect. Were parents too busy to attend? Did they not want to admit to being overtaxed? In any case, "stress reduction" wasn't a compelling subject for them.

Practicing mindfulness has many benefits beyond reducing stress. My own parenting profited greatly from incorporating it. I wondered whether teaching parents how they could use mindfulness to support their children would fly. This thought was the genesis of the new, well-attended workshop described below:

The Joy of Mindful Parenting

Presence is the key ingredient of all mindful parenting, staying fully present both to oneself and to one's children. In this workshop we will engage in contemplative exercises that enhance awareness of our thoughts and feelings, sharpen sensory awareness, and promote mindful speech and deep listening. These skills are important building blocks and nourish rewarding relationships with both children and adults.

To provide extra motivation for parents to attend, I told my math students that I guaranteed their parents would benefit. A number of those who showed up were parents of those students.

Sometimes conditions in the moment provide all the motivation that's needed. In *The Art of Possibility* by Benjamin and Rosamund Stone Zander,[17] the authors included a fascinating chapter titled "Giving an A." In it they described wrestling with the problem of motivating Benjamin's talented students to take risks when performing at the highly competitive New England Conservatory of Music. The night before the first day of classes, the Zanders came up with a radical proposal which Professor Zander then presented to his students. He promised them all grades of A in the course if they wrote and turned in to him letters dated at the course's conclusion. In their letters, Zander asked them to describe the person and musician they'd have become by the end of the school year. On receiving the letters, Professor Zander's role changed. He was no longer the judge of their worthiness. He became their cheerleader, helping them realize their dreams.

I was inspired to adapt Professor Zander's letter and simply ask all my math students to write what they'd accomplish by the end of the year. Not surprisingly, some students included on their lists a math grade of A. More helpful to me were their descriptions of improvements in areas like class participation and attention to homework, changes which justified their A's.

Several days later we were stupefied by the events of 9/11. Back-to-School Night at the Upper School was scheduled for 9/13. Our Principal decided to hold it as planned. My aim in the past had been to give parents a sense of my goals for their youngsters and how I would be assisting them. Mostly this was an opportunity for parents to meet me. This time, because of the letters my students had written, I knew much more about their own goals. I also knew that in the tragic aftermath of 9/11 all of us were terribly worried about our children. Here was a teachable moment, a chance to support parents. I decided not to talk about math. Instead I shared with these parents about the letter writing their students had done the previous week. I then handed out school letterhead and envelopes, invited parents to address envelopes to themselves and to write letters dated the following June. I suggested they begin their letters, "Dear Me, I feel proud of the job I have done with my parenting this year. I've grown as a parent in the following ways... with these results..." Engrossed, they finished their letters, sealed the envelopes, and handed them back to me to mail the following June. Only one parent, a solo dad, sat at his desk and wrote nothing. How did my lesson connect with this dad? I had no idea. Had there been time afterwards, I would have asked him.

REFLECTIONS AND CONTEMPLATIONS

My first two parent workshops focused on self-care, the third on awareness and communication. Contemplate a time when self-care, awareness, or communication was important in your own growth.

Write about it.

Recall an experience of a teachable moment as a teacher. As a student.

What stands out in the way you responded?

Recall a time when you experienced seeing yourself as the person you wanted to become. Take some time to go back to that experience and dwell with it.

Where did it lead?

LIGHTING FIRES

My first mentor, David Mallery, was a master fire builder and his annual by-invitation-only Westtown Seminar on Teaching—Westtown for short—was his masterwork. Luckily, I attended this one-week gathering following my second year of teaching at Sidwell Friends. The first day we participated in Project Adventure outdoor challenges. Soon we were all being introduced to aikido, theater games, and inclusive language. The experience was so energizing that newfound friends and I discussed its potential to forestall burnout for some of our colleagues. However, when we looked around, we saw no evidence of it. David had only invited educators who sparkled.

All of us had just completed an intense year of teaching. The first evening David's job was simply to rekindle flames from glowing embers. Enter David's friend Willi Unsoeld, one of the first Americans to summit Everest. We sat spellbound listening to Willi's account of his preparation and ascent while watching slides with spectacular views. Out we went into the night when it was over, carrying a sense of the immensity of their challenge as well as the determination of the climbing team inside us. During the following week we'd be preparing for our own climbs at our schools back home.

Several years later, David gathered a very different group for his Administrator's Life Conference. Although I had no administrative responsibilities, David invited me to attend. This conference occurred in the midst of the school year, many of the participants coming for a much-needed break. Some additional fuel was called for. David, always the master, divided us into small groups and asked us to reflect on the most powerful life experiences we'd had. After some time dwelling with these experiences and writing in our journals, we met in our small groups. Long-buried energy was unleashed. Two members of my group related very moving war-time experiences. I told of a night sitting with my brain-damaged, younger brother hemorrhaging in a small island hospital, awaiting the arrival of plasma on the morning plane. When our sharing concluded, we were renewed, ready for whatever would follow.

Finding a way to pass some of David's fire on to young people turned out to be easier than I'd anticipated. Within a week of returning home from Westtown, I was invited to join the staff of St. Mary's Center for Interdisciplinary Studies later that summer. The Center offered a two-week residential program for state of Maryland gifted and talented junior high school students. When animated film-maker Bonnie Willette described the rich program that Director Jay McTighe had inaugurated the previous year, I felt a strong res-onance with my own Westtown experience. Students were invited to choose two of the Center's four, week-long courses and spend five and a half hours a day engaged in one of these dynamic avenues of learning—Cultural and Historical Explorations, Environmental Science, Mathematics, and Artistic and Creative Expression. That summer I taught Mathematics. To me, it felt like school all over again. The following eight summers I taught Problem Solving. I was able to challenge our students to explore uncharted territory— exciting for them and invigorating for me.

Of the Center's entire teachings, my all-time favorite event occurred the first day of Artistic and Creative Expressions (ACE). These course instructors were skilled in fiber arts, poetry, film-making, instrumental music, and theater. They had reviewed stu-dent portfolios and program applications and accepted students whose work seemed exceptional. However, polished work wasn't the point of ACE; rather, it was to engage in a creative process, and, for students used to plying practiced talents, this could feel risky. At their first meeting, ACE instructors greeted the group and launched the course:

> "Welcome to Artistic and Creative Expression. We know you've been looking forward to working in a particular area of the arts. Tomorrow you'll be able to choose one to focus

on for the remainder of the week. Today we'll work as an ensemble to write and produce an opera. We'll perform it in the lobby of the Arts Center at 3:00 p.m. this afternoon. Any questions? Let's go…"

I was privileged to attend such an opera and share the exuberance of its creators. This project ignited the students. Their camaraderie set the stage for the more individually focused work in the four days that followed.

In addition to doing coursework, St. Mary's students met every evening in multi-age coed groups for activities with counselors. Counselors, who often returned year after year, engaged students in lively discussions on such topics as: What does it feel like to be singled out as gifted and talented? What does peer pressure look like for you? How would you describe your boy/girl relationships? An awareness of consensus decision-making seemed to feed the social/emotional needs of these gifted early adolescents. For many, these evening meetings broke new ground, providing many with a safe peer group to explore more openly who they were. The students were totally engaged throughout the day.

Learning doesn't always go that way. Sometimes a flame thrower is needed to light a fire under a student. Once that student was me. At Woodrow Wilson, where I began my teaching career, only grades went home to student families. At Sidwell Friends, we gave grades and comments. I labored over my comments, wanting them to be useful as well as descriptive. As a result, I often turned in grades and comments late. Eventually the Assistant Principal stepped in:

"Richard," she said, the tone of her voice underscoring her message, "this will be the last time you turn your grades in late." I felt threatened.

"Or else?" I asked.

"There is no '*Or else*,'" she replied.

This confrontation shook me up. Wasn't I a team player? I needed to call on my self-discipline. Never again was I late with class grades and comments. In fact, I began to complete my comments early, offering students a chance to read them before I handed them in. I asked students for written feedback. Was there anything I'd perceived incorrectly? Was there anything important I'd failed to mention? Sometimes I edited my comments, incorporating a student's feedback. When a student pointed out that I'd failed to mention improvement in an area of their focus, I understood them better. This was a grand opportunity for students to assess themselves and for me to honor the role of dialogue in true education.

REFLECTIONS AND CONTEMPLATIONS

Contemplate someone who lit a fire in your life.

What qualities did this person have?

How did you relate to this person?

How have you lit fires in others?

VIGOR

An old adage says, *When the student is ready, the teacher will appear.*
So it was for me at David Mallery's Administrator's Life workshop where I was profoundly moved by the presentation of his
friend, Paula Lawrence Wehmiller. Ten years later, I heard Paula
speak at the National Cathedral. In the interim she'd ordained as
an Episcopal priest. Reconnecting, I was excited to hear she was
offering spiritual direction for teachers. I asked for her business
card. A few years later, as I began sharing mindfulness in schools,
I needed some support. I was creating programs effectively, but I
needed assistance in seeing the big picture and how I fit into it. I
contacted Paula, and we set up monthly phone calls. She would
listen for half an hour, then ask me questions, share a relevant poem
or tell me a story from her life that illuminated just where in this
latest adventure I found myself. I felt privileged and grateful.

Difficulties seemed to arise a day or two before our scheduled
calls. On one occasion I'd just received a rejection message from
Claudia Gallant, program director of the annual conference of the
National Association of Independent Schools. My friend Irene
McHenry and I had submitted a proposal to offer a mindfulness
workshop at the 2004 conference. Claudia believed a contemplative offering was at odds with the character of the conference. I
spoke with Paula the next day.

"I understand how suggesting that pupils just sit and breathe
when their parents are paying thousands of dollars for schooling
might not be well received," I told her. "But, if we've perceived
this leading correctly, our proposal should have been accepted."
Way would open as Quakers say. "All my life way has opened—
the way I became a teacher, my arrival at Sidwell Friends, how I

taught at St. Mary's, landing at Pendle Hill where I met Elisabeth, my future partner, and discovered Thich Nhat Hanh."

"That isn't my understanding of a leading," Paula replied. She then described her calling to the priesthood, how she'd found seminary demanding at every turn but knew she *had* to finish. Seminary was a challenge she could not *not* take. "Is your workshop a challenge you cannot not take?" she asked.

Without thinking, I replied, "No! We have to do it!"

"Then contact the woman who sent you the message." Paula responded, "and tell her she's made a mistake."

Her words, like a sunrise, illuminated the darkness that had settled around me.

A week later I was drinking tea with Claudia Gallant at a café near Sidwell and saying, "The contemplative nature of our proposed workshop certainly contrasts sharply with the busy, intense nature of the conference and the nature of many of your member schools as well." I stopped speaking for a moment, letting my words sink into the space between us. Then I continued. "That is why it is *so* important. Educators need to learn how to slow down and be completely present to their colleagues, their students and themselves." Claudia got it. She not only reversed her decision, she also added a contemplative track to the conference, reserving a room for early morning meditation, silent meals, and quiet time. What a lesson in trusting my own leadings!

We typically categorize motivation as intrinsic or extrinsic. But motivation or fire building is far more complex. In any situation there are numerous factors that support or inhibit motivation for each individual. Intrinsic factors can be relational as in the case of parents wanting to improve their parenting. Extrinsic factors can connect deeply with the individual as in the case of students doing yoga to do better in math. Fear may be involved—fear of poor results, fear of disapproval—also its opposites—courage and agency. In a given situation there may be conflicting supporting and inhibiting factors. This was the case in the summer of 1973 when I attended an institute for math teachers at the University of Indiana.

On the first day of class our Mathematical Models professor informed us that our grades would be determined by two sets of problems and a take-home final exam. The course was ill-suited for a group of junior and senior high math lacking mathematical sophistication. In addition to this, after returning our first problem sets, the professor told us he'd found evidence of collusion. He threatened giving each of us an oral final exam if he found similar signs on the second set. Student anger boiled. Our professor was giving us a take-home lesson on how *not* to teach.

With a strong mathematics background, I found most of the professor's problems straightforward. However, on the second set I became engrossed in analyzing a mathematical model of the learning process. Having left myself two days to complete the work, I finished half the problems on the first day. The last four looked standard but tedious. The next day I began work on the model and discovered a subtlety that would require a great deal of time to investigate adequately. Focused like a laser, I devoted the entire day to the solution, foregoing the last three problems. The professor's problem had become mine, my high school paper on Socrates all over again. I turned the answers in along with an explanation of my choice to go for maximum learning. I received full credit for my analysis, almost full credit on the first four problems, and none for the last three. My top standing in the class fell to below average.

Two weeks before the end of the course, I sustained a broken collarbone in a motorcycle accident and stayed in the hospital for a day. There I had time to think. I made the decision to stop attending Mathematical Models. I didn't work on the take-home exam. When I opened my grade report a few weeks later, I found an "incomplete." My decision to withdraw from Mathematical Models was freeing, an important moment in my own growth. I wrote informing the university, "If I ever completed a course in my life, it was this one. I decided I was finished." Failing the course didn't faze me. I'd satisfied my own criteria.

I don't hold grades in high regard either as a means of evaluation or of motivation. However, in Sidwell Friends Upper School courses they were required. Grades tell students and parents little about students' strengths and weaknesses, yet the stark appearance of an emotionally-laden letter grade on a teacher's report frequently overshadows the teacher's comments. I found the same true of grades on tests, whether assigned with letters or numbers.

This changed in the spring of 1982 when Sidwell's Middle School Principal, Harry Finks, invited me to teach Math I to a group of precocious eighth graders the following year. Math

I was the honors ninth-grade algebra course. I'd been teaching Math I to ninth graders and knew how challenging it was. The eighth graders would be bright but unfamiliar with the rigor of an Upper School course. Since Middle School teachers weren't required to grade their students, I was overjoyed to dispense with grades. I knew these eighth graders would need time to learn how to study Math I to be able to enjoy success. The reports I would send to parents would describe where students were doing well and which areas needed more attention. My intention would be to focus on learning, not evaluation.

Weekly Meeting for Worship in the Quaker tradition helped ground the fast-paced Upper School life. For forty minutes on Thursday mornings, students and faculty sat in a silence punctuated by an occasional spontaneous sharing. The following fall, during the first of our Upper School Meetings, I reflected on appreciating my grade of C from Mr. Boyle in senior English and my choosing to follow my curiosity and accept the consequences at Indiana University's summer school. In both cases I managed not to get caught up in earning high grades but dove for a deeper level of learning. Now I could offer my students a look inward for the same satisfaction, as well as outward for mathematical achievement.

I found myself trembling in the silence, a sure sign I'd been given a message to share. I rose and expressed my overwhelming gratitude at finally teaching without grades. After twelve years, my students and I would truly experience the joy of learning math for math's sake. I only wished it were possible in my Upper School classes as well.

While I gave no grades, I was responsible for placing students in the appropriate Upper School math course, honors or regular tenth-grade geometry. Only once did this prove a problem. A mother called to share her son's upset on learning he'd not been placed in the honors class. "Joe told me he would have worked harder if he'd had any idea he wasn't doing well. If you're willing to postpone your decision until Math I ends, he'd like to prove to you that he belongs in Math II." Had anyone in Joe's family read my comments delineating the many areas that needed Joe's attention? I wondered. Was a grade necessary? Joe did work harder and went on to take honors math courses in the Upper School. There his lack of internal motivation contributed to a mediocre career.

Concerned as I was about student motivation, I seldom reflected on my own. This changed in the winter of 1999–2000 when I read *The Seven Stages of Money Maturity*[18] by George Kinder. His stage called *vigor* got my attention. Kinder explained that work contains vigor if it returns as much or more energy as you put into it—if it has a volitional quality. He then invited his readers to meditate on work experiences that had had this quality. Three immediately came to mind—teaching at St. Mary's, teaching Math I to eighth-graders, and conducting a senior seminar on conflict resolution at Sidwell. Did my math teaching have *vigor*? I enjoyed it, I did a good job, and I had no signs of burnout. At the end of each year, however, I was tired. Summer vacation was where I recharged my batteries. I saw I could continue in this vein until I retired, but did I want to? Did I want to go for *vigor*? Excited by my realization, I made an appointment to talk with Headmaster Bruce Stewart. I explained that I wanted to refresh my spiritual life by taking a one-year leave of absence. Bruce asked if I planned to return the following year. I said yes, but honestly I had no idea whether a year away would change my mind.

As spring wore on with no plans for my leave, I started to feel uneasy. What if the next year passed and I discovered no passion? I got the idea to go to Parker Palmer's new Center for Teacher Formation, an outgrowth of his seminal book *The Courage to Teach: Exploring the Inner Landscape of a Teacher's Life*.[19] I could train there to be a facilitator. When I told her, my partner Elisabeth responded, "That's Parker's work, Richard. You need to find your own work." Ta-da! I knew she was right. I continued to live with uncertainty, awaiting clarity. Later that spring my friend Sue-Anne called from upstate New York to lament the tremendous pressures experienced by students and teachers.

"Someone ought to teach them meditation," I told her. As the words came out of my mouth, I knew that someone was me. I'd discovered my new direction! I could begin immediately by offering mindfulness retreats to teachers.

REFLECTIONS AND CONTEMPLATIONS

Recall a time when you enjoyed work with vigor.

Contemplate a significant experience you've had with external motivation.

With internal motivation.

What conditions contributed to these experiences?

What did you learn from them?

NOTES

1 Thurman, H. (2010). On *The living wisdom of Howard Thurman: A visionary for our time.* Colorado: Sounds True, Inc.
2 Holt, J. (1964). *How children fail.* New York: Pitman.
3 Wolfe, T. (1929). *Look homeward angel: A story of the buried life.* New York: Charles Scribner's Sons.
4 Auden, W.H. (1930). "Petition," in *Poems.* London: Faber and Faber.
5 Salinger, J.D. (1951). *The catcher in the rye.* Boston: Little Brown and Co.
6 Hanh, T.N. (1993). *The blooming of a lotus: Guided meditation exercises for healing and transformation.* Boston: Beacon Press, 21.
7 I describe this teaching and my preparation leading up to it in Brady, Richard (2007), "Learning to Stop, Stopping to Learn: Discovering the Contemplative Dimension in Education," *Journal of Transformative Education* 5, no 4, 372–94.
8 X, M. and Haley, A. (2015). *The Autobiography of Malcolm X.* New York: Ishi Press, 35.
9 Eliot. T.S. (1991). From "Little Gidding," in *Collected poems, 1909–1962.* New York: Harcourt Brace, 207.
10 Suresha, R. (2011). *The uncommon sense of the Immortal Nasrudin: Stories, jokes, and donkey tales for the beloved Persian folk hero.* Danbury, CT: Bear Bones Books, 30.
11 Estés, C.P. (1996). *Women who run with the wolves: Myths and stories of the wild woman archetype.* New York: Ballantine Books, 163.
12 John Fitzgerald Kennedy. Inaugural Address. January 20, 1961.
13 McCourt, F. (2005). *Teacher man: A memoir.* New York: Scribner.
14 Hanh, T.N. (1993). *The blooming of a lotus: Guided meditation exercises for healing and transformation.* Boston: Beacon Press, 23.
15 The Mindfulness in Education Network's website, accessed October 29, 2020, is http://www.mindfuled.org.
16 Scattergood, M. (2009). "Beanie Baby Meditation," in *Tuning in: Mindfulness in teaching and learning,* eds. Irene McHenry and Richard Brady. Philadelphia: Friends Council on Education, 33–6.
17 Zander, R.S. and Zander, B. (2000). *The art of possibility: Transforming professional and personal life.* Boston: Harvard Business School Press.
18 Kinder, G. (1999). *The seven stages of money maturity: Understanding the spirit and value of money in your life.* New York: Dell.
19 Palmer, P. (1998). *The courage to teach: Exploring the inner landscape of a teacher's life.* San Francisco: Jossey-Bass.

PART II

LIVING WITHOUT BOUNDARIES

What is your greatest ambition in life? To become immortal
… and then die.

—Jean-Luc Godard[1]

Boundaries are nonexistent for newborns. As they become conscious of their needs, they continue living in the present moment. By about age two, children have for the most part become aware that some behaviors can have negative consequences. They learn that misbehavior brings disciplinary responses, initially at home, later at school. Poor schoolwork results in low grades. Friends become important and influence decisions about how to act. As children lose the freedom they once enjoyed, they may also lose their sense of agency. Some of the following stories describe my confrontations with boundaries from high school on. Others are devoted to ways I and colleagues nurtured agency and freedom. These didn't come without risk and possible negative consequences, but all contributed to significant learning. The most profound learning experiences I've witnessed occurred when students or adults, working together, went beyond independence and encountered interdependence.

Boundaries are intimately connected with expectations. How many of our actions are determined by the expectations of others? How and when do we learn to trust ourselves? To look inward for answers? For direction? Before becoming a high school teacher myself, I had two significant experiences in high school of what Quakers call following my inner guide. One was rejecting my parents' advice that I transfer out of Mr. Boyle's senior English class, the other writing a paper on Socrates "for myself" in Mr. Boyle's class. As a student in Indiana University's summer programs, I chose to forgo working on some assigned problems in order to devote myself fully to what had become a completely absorbing learning experience for me, in other words, "my problem."

How these actions arose in me, I can't say. I did develop a sense of self-confidence in English classes that was nurtured by my eleventh-grade teacher Mr. Landers, as well as an ease with mathematics due to my success over the years with the subject. However, experiences of turning inward to find responses were not part of any curriculum I'd ever encountered. On the contrary, teachers always played the central role. What was it they were looking for from me?

In my final years of teaching, changing this picture was a prime motivation for my decision never to read what students wrote in the backs of their journals. By year's end, they'd written a generous amount there. Naturally, I was curious. I decided to ask students to take their journals home for a night, read all the entries in the back, select one that seemed significant, and write a one-page paper about it for me. I saw from these papers that their journaling had borne much fruit. One paper stood out. The writer reported on an entry he'd written in mid-November. Reading his entries chronologically, he'd discovered that this was the first time he'd written for himself rather than for an assignment. I was surprised. He was so accustomed to writing for teachers, it took him two months to discover how to write for himself. Not only had his motivation changed; he was aware of the change.

I'd been teaching thirty-five years before I began giving my math students journals. In that time my understanding of education had changed significantly. The shift was due in large part to mentors and fortuitous educational experiences like attending the Westtown Seminar. Most of the participants at Westtown were schoolteachers and administrators. A few notable exceptions included Juma, then Kuwait's Minister of Education, who had visited Sidwell several weeks before but now wore blue jeans. Another was James, my Westtown roommate.

After dropping out of college, James began working in a fast-food restaurant. When I asked him what brought him to Westtown, James told me his mom, a school counselor and former Westtown participant, had asked David if her son could show a film at Westtown—one she'd produced about his identity crisis as a teen. While attending the conference, James hoped to discover for himself the purpose of education. I watched him share his collection of rocks, sing his original songs, accompany himself on guitar, and invite all of us to stargaze through his telescope. As our week ended, I told James that he embodied for me the educated person, exactly what I hoped my students would become. Who they became, not what they knew, was at the heart of my thinking. James brought his learning to life and shared it generously with all of us. The stimulus came from inside him, not from the opinions or curricula of others.

Some years later I came upon a poem by Sufi poet Jalāl ad-Dīn Muhammad Rūmī that beautifully expresses what I would have enjoyed conveying to James. It became one of the prompts I used for my math students—inviting them to contemplate and write on. How I wished I'd been able to see what they wrote!

Two Kinds of Intelligence

There are two kinds of intelligence: one acquired,
as a child in school memorizes facts and concepts
from books and from what the teacher says,
collecting information from the traditional sciences
as well as from the new sciences.

With such intelligence you rise in the world.
You get ranked ahead or behind others
in regard to your competence in retaining
information. You stroll with this intelligence
in and out of fields of knowledge, getting always more
marks on your preserving tablets.

There is another kind of tablet, one
already completed and preserved inside you.
A spring overflowing its springbox. A freshness
in the center of the chest. This other intelligence
does not turn yellow or stagnate. It's fluid,
and it doesn't move from outside to inside
through the conduits of plumbing-learning.

This second knowing is a fountainhead
from within you, moving out.[2]

Developing ways to help students find and value this second kind of intelligence in a culture so focused on the first kind was an ongoing challenge for me. I knew it was at the core of who I was as a teacher.

REFLECTIONS AND CONTEMPLATIONS

Contemplate an experience you've had of following your inner guide.

What stands out about this experience?

What did you learn?

How have you nurtured your inner intelligence?

How have you nourished the inner intelligence of your students?

NEW KINDS OF TEACHING

My career as a math teacher began in 1970 with a three-year stretch at Woodrow Wilson High School, a Washington, DC public school near Sidwell Friends. Unlike Sidwell, Wilson was a school with every sort of diversity imaginable. Student families from many countries and many rungs on the economic ladder sent their youngsters there. They came with a wide range of abilities and preparation. As a first-year teacher, I felt fortunate to end up teaching four sections of Geometry as well as the Advanced Placement Calculus course. Neither attendance nor attention were problems in these classes. I'd studied math and physics in college and graduate school, but had taken no education courses. I taught in much the same way I'd been taught—spend time going over the previous night's homework, explain the new lesson, sometimes have an opportunity to begin working on the new assignment. This was what I knew. I had a lot to learn.

During my first year of teaching, I discovered my passion for improving education. I have no doubt this came from my mother. She was one of the most creative people I knew, always noticing opportunities to contribute to life. Mother started two businesses. One was a talking book and record company where she recorded drama students reading children's stories, then packaged the records with the storybooks. Her second business manufactured picture frames with easily removable backs, enabling parents and teachers to easily display their children's latest artwork. That first year of teaching, I also discovered Harold Jacobs' revolutionary new textbook, *Mathematics: A Human Endeavor*[3] at a math conference. I immediately recognized its potential as an exciting option to traditional general mathematics texts. Liberally filled with cartoons and photos, Jacobs' text proffered clear explanations of major mathematical topics and compelling problems that reviewed basic numeracy skills. Inspired by it, I received permission to develop and teach *Topics in Mathematics* the following year as a final mathematics course for less able students. Because many of the students attended irregularly, the course had to be self-paced. This was only possible because *Human Endeavor* could be read and understood by all the students. I thrived on helping these young people take responsibility for their own learning and grow in the process. In the spring my Principal told me the DC Public Schools Central Office had informed him that my students wouldn't be receiving credit. "Topics in Mathematics" didn't exist on their course roster. "Please ask them to add it," I replied. He did so. They added it. Crisis averted. I felt empowered.

In order for a second year of teaching at Wilson to be available to me, I needed to take two education courses and become fully certified to teach in DC Public Schools. Looking forward to teaching Topics in the fall, I braced myself for the summer offering, a course called Methods and Principles of Secondary Education at the University of Maryland. I was in for a big surprise. The instructor, Ron McKeen, greeted us, holding up a book: "This is our textbook. We won't be using it." Down on the desk it went. Pulling out a newspaper, he read aloud an op-ed piece on the new amendment granting 18-year-olds the right to vote. He then invited our responses. This turned out to be typical Ron, introducing a think-piece on education, theory, or current events as a springboard for reflection and discussion.

The course was a joint venture between teacher and students from start to finish. Near the end, we split up into groups to work on projects of our own design which we'd present to the class. Inspired by a music teacher, our group employed the Orff method of spontaneous experimentation to teach music-making to the rest of the class. What a scene! Sitting in a large circle on the floor holding percussion instruments, there we were listening, responding, and improvising. A class member spontaneously established a beat. Others picked it up. Soon we heard new strands weave in and out, sounds rising and falling. The music was no less than our experience of life. In this rich classroom environment we had no papers, tests, quizzes, or exams. We drew our grades from a hat. They were all A's. Grades, having never been mentioned, had no impact on our learning. Inspired by Ron's class, a new curiosity opened inside me. I began pouring through books on alternative education. I made my way from Postman and Weingartner's *Teaching as a Subversive Activity*[4] to A.S. Neill's *Summerhill*[5] and Paulo Freire's *Pedagogy of the Oppressed.*[6] In different ways, each of these books painted pictures in which students co-created their education along with their teachers.

During Ron's course we were confronted by the question of what education meant. Was learning essentially what we made it? In the classroom, we shared our joy, anger, humor, and frustration. Each of us had a chance to make a unique offering which was received in as many ways as there were students. Each person contributed simultaneously as student and teacher. We sprouted like a spring garden. The course brought out every aspect of creativity I'd ever known. We asked questions, challenged accepted truths, played with ideas, tried out new roles, created our own philosophies, joked, took risks, and analyzed what was happening. As in photosynthesis in the natural world, everything of importance flowed from this process or was incorporated into it. Prior to this experience, I'd never known creativity to flower so thoroughly within a given context. Here ingenuity created its own context. The medium was the message.

Inspired by my summer with Ron, I began my second year of teaching at Woodrow Wilson looking for ways to empower students. In addition to Topics in Mathematics and AP Calculus, I was delighted to be assigned the advanced pre-calculus class. I wanted to promote student independence in my advanced courses as well as in Topics, so I invited the students in the advanced courses to determine their own grades. At the beginning of the semester, they let me know how much weight they'd be placing on homework, class participation, quizzes, tests, exams, and other factors. At the end of the semester they'd meet with me again to explain how they'd come up with their grades. Karl, the best mathematician in the pre-calculus class, told me he'd determine his grade based on how much he learned. "Wonderful!" I said. "How will I know if the grade you determine is appropriate?" "You'll have to trust me," replied Karl. Some years later, when I began handing out journals to students, I realized I could have asked Karl to keep a journal of what he was learning. I had to smile. By this time, Karl had won the Cole Prize awarded every three years by the American Mathematical Society for the best work in number theory.

After three years of teaching at Wilson, it was time for me to find new sources of inspiration. When Sidwell Friends hired me, I was pleased to learn I'd be teaching primarily geometry, my favorite subject both as a high school student and as a teacher. The geometry text then in use at Sidwell was a good source of problems, but not especially readable for average students. I asked Naomi Darrigrand, Math Department chair and teacher of the other geometry sections, if I could use Harold Jacobs' new geometry book. With Jacobs' trademark humor and fresh-ness, his text presented geometry in an understandable way. This would make it possible for me to do less explaining and more facilitating. The prospect of juniors using a book filled with cartoons didn't sit well with Naomi, but my faith in Jacobs' book was so great that I pressed my case. Naomi relented. When school began, I was surprised to see her students also using Jacobs' book. She must have changed her mind, I thought. But when I inquired, Naomi explained, "Students sometimes need to change sections, so it's best for all of us to use the same book."

Soon after classes began, parents came to meet teachers. This was my first Back-to-School Night. In one geometry section, a father openly disapproved of the Jacobs book, declaring it failed to cover the geometry he'd learned as a high school student. Naomi's concerns had materialized. I was taken aback. Before I could col-lect myself, another father vehemently disagreed, saying "The material is completely in line with the geometry I studied." The second father's tacit approval of my approach restored my compo-sure and boosted my confidence in my inner guide. Without that, how could I ask my students to trust their own inner intelligence?

I'd only been teaching this geometry course for a couple of years when I was invited to participate on a geometry panel at a local math teachers' conference. The two other panel members were experienced teachers who used traditional textbooks and whose pedagogy was teacher-centered. Awaiting for our panel to begin, I felt uneasy. I'd never spoken to a room full of math teachers. I lacked experience. What did I really have to say? Going outside I sat on a bench and breathed in fresh spring air. I believed strongly in what I was doing. I believed strongly in Harold Jacobs' way of approaching the teaching of mathematics. Others could benefit from hearing my experience. I went back inside, now connected with myself, and connected with the audience; I spoke with conviction about promoting student agency. It was that simple.

My admiration for Harold Jacobs was so great that when I later learned he'd be speaking at a regional math conference in Washington, I ordered a dozen red roses delivered to his hotel room. The note with them read, "With great appreciation for your work from your friends at Sidwell Friends School." His books promoted student independence, transforming their experience as learners—a great contribution to mathematics education. They also made math understandable, interesting, and fun. During the conference, I had the opportunity to thank Mr. Jacobs in person. What a joy! By then his geometry book had become a faithful companion. Whenever I opened it, it evoked an inner smile.

REFLECTIONS AND CONTEMPLATIONS

What or who was your inspiration for becoming an educator?

Recall a meaningful experience you had as a new teacher.

What did you learn from it about teaching? About yourself?

RISK AND SAFETY

Taking risks and exploring new territory were not regular features of my life. My mother did fly with her cousin in his two-seater airplane when she was twenty-five, but when my father found out, he told her never to do it again. He was a Jewish refugee from Germany. I inherited many habits of safety and control from him. These affected my personal relationships and occasionally made appearances in educational settings, even in the warm and caring environment of the Westtown Seminar.

Toward the end of our Westtown week, Shirley, an English teacher from California, presented a poetry writing workshop. She began by inviting us to close our eyes, review our Westtown experience, and locate one special moment that held great energy for us. Here's what came up for me:

> We're walking along the top of a three-foot-high brick wall, and we come to a four-foot gap. Willi, the leader of our 'joy walk,' asks us to stop and decide whether the person behind us should be permitted to jump across the gap. When I turn around, I see immediately behind me Juma, the Minister of Education from Kuwait. I'm uneasy about taking the leap, but I want to jump. Juma looks anxious about jumping, and my intuition tells me not to give him my permission. During the next several minutes, we see a member of our group miss the landing, fall and cut her leg open on a brick. Waiting my turn, I think about a passage in Norman Mailer's The Naked and the Dead,[7] where a weak soldier falls to his death. When I finally land on the other side, I relax. Watching Juma step

down, walk past the gap, then step up on the wall again, I wonder about the decision for him I made so quickly. Should we have talked about his feelings? Perhaps he wanted to jump? Did I make the choice for him too soon? I took the risk of jumping, but I didn't give Juma the chance. Moving so quickly, I'd not given myself room for feeling the growing tension between risk and safety.

Recalling all this and feeling the unsettledness in my body, I rose. The energy moved me around the room. Returning to my seat, I picked up some crayons and captured the moment on paper. Then a poem gushed out.

The inner voice
Resounds, "No!"
No questions are asked.
Something this clear
Surely comes
From intuition.
But might it possibly
Be fear—
Fear of risk,
Responsibility,
Fear even to look
Fear
In the face?

Reconciling risk and safety was an ongoing issue for me. Not surprisingly, opportunities arose at St. Mary's.

Given his German-Jewish heritage, control was important to my father. It was predictable that letting go would also be problematic for me. One summer at St. Mary's I received a powerful lesson about control and letting go. I'd offered my class a murder mystery to crack. At the onset, each student received one or two written clues. The rules were simple. Students could read their clues at any time and offer their clues to others at any time, but they couldn't take others' clues or even ask for them. One young man held onto his clue and to those that were given him. Without the clues he held tight to his vest, it became clear to the rest of the group that there was no way they could find the killer. Slowly, slowly all the class members passed that student their clues. He sat in a quandary, attempting to solve the mystery alone. But he couldn't. Ultimately, he gave up and handed all his clues to a student next to him. She then wisely distributed them to the rest of the class. In short order, they solved the mystery. The clue-holder was likely one of his school's top students who may never have needed help before and didn't know how to ask for it. That young man could have been me, feeling I was the one on whom responsibility lay and not knowing how to take the risk of trusting others.

Risk has many dimensions. One is taking on challenges you're not prepared for. Awareness of such risks accompanied ACE's weekly opera productions and played an important role one year for the Center as a whole. Each year at St. Mary's the ACE instructors chose a theme for their course. This theme was then used in designing that year's Center T-shirt. All of us explored ways to incorporate the annual theme. In later years, the entire faculty chose the theme for the following summer. We used topics designed to inspire learning like *connections* and *reflections*. But wouldn't our students discover these aspects of learning back home? St. Mary's contributed its unique approach. I'd been particularly aware of challenges our students in Problem Solving faced. Most of these bright youngsters were unaccustomed to difficulty. I suggested we adopt the theme *uncertainty*, an idea which at first our director, Jay, dismissed out of hand. "You expect me to tell parents who are entrusting their 12-year-olds to us for two weeks that the camp's theme is 'uncertainty'?" A month before the program started, he wrote the staff:

This year's theme is *UNCERTAINTY*. I must admit that I had a negative reaction to it when first proposed. I had a difficult time "deferring judgment." As we discussed *UNCERTAINTY* along with other possibilities at the Instructional Planning Weekend, I became more and more intrigued with the idea. Unlike themes of past years, uncertainty creates a certain tension; uncertainty motivates me to think deeply. I am now a convert ... and excited about our topic. I now feel, along with many other staff members, that this may be our most challenging theme to date.[8]

I, too, was excited to be launching the summer with such a compelling theme. On the first day we distributed "uncertainty journals" to students enrolled in Problem Solving. At the end of each day they were invited to record their uncertainties. The problems we'd given them were unlike any they'd encountered before—from finding mathematical patterns to protecting a raw egg, dropped from a one-meter height. Solutions often required collaboration and took time to formulate. With journals in hand and time to write, students began to fathom how uncertainty was an ingredient in problem solving. I also kept a journal, recording my uncertainties about teaching. Could I have done a better job presenting a problem? Did I give students enough time to work alone before forming small groups? If this course reduced our anxiety about uncertainty and risk taking, it would deliver a great boon for all of us to take home.

Sometimes surprising opportunities to take risks presented themselves. One involved an extracurricular activity at Sidwell. During my first years there, I wasn't known so much as a math teacher but as the coach of the school's team for the TV show *It's Academic*, the world's longest-running TV quiz show. Having coached Wilson's team my last year there, it seemed natural to fill the same role at Sidwell. Our team got as far as the city championships my first year and the semi-finals the next. I spent hours at the Library of Congress collecting questions to use in practice. I drove our team to other schools to compete in scrimmages. We hosted scrimmages at Sidwell.

When our administration announced that teachers who chose to coach would begin receiving stipends, I wrote the Principal to request one for coaching *It's Academic*. I cited the time and energy I spent, sometimes through all three sports seasons. He denied my request, clarifying that the stipends were intended only to encourage teachers to coach sports teams. Since coaching *It's Academic* was no longer the priority it had once been for me, I decided to retire from coaching.

A few summers later at St. Mary's I received a surprise call from Clint Wilkins, the current Sidwell Principal. He'd been unable to fill an unexpected vacancy for the *It's Academic* coach. Would I come out of retirement for a year? I took time to reflect. Each year a number of students interested in making the team attended practices. As the first match approached and I selected our three-person team, most of the seniors and some of the younger students lost interest. and competitive practices fizzled out. The teams were always comprised of three boys. Only a few girls ever tried out. None ever made the team. Few folks besides friends and families of the three team members were likely to attend any of the TV tapings. Did I want to commit that much time and effort to something that contributed so narrowly to the school?

Several days later I called Clint, laid out my concerns, and proposed a solution:

> I'd like to name students to two teams—a first-round team and a second-round team with different students. Should both teams win, all-stars will represent us in the semi-final. This approach will keep twice as many students engaged in practice, increase the chances for female team members, and expand the number of friends and family members attending our TV tapings.

"If the students who want to be on the team approve your plan, I will," Clint replied.

That fall the students approved a modified version of my plan. They wanted Dan Singer, Sidwell's superstar, on both teams. After our first-round team won, I was certain the producers were puzzled when I told them a different team would compete in the next round. Team two came close to winning. It was a memorable season. We celebrated with the first-ever team dinner at Yenching Palace, owned then by a team member's family. Afterwards I retired for good. Risking our chances of success by not fielding our three strongest competitors, we'd made a compelling statement for inclusion.

REFLECTIONS AND CONTEMPLATIONS

Recall a time when you chose to take a risk or a time when you chose not to.

What did you learn?

Explore the landscape of uncertainty in your own experience.

Was there a time in your life when you welcomed uncertainty as part of your learning?

What was that like?

FREEDOM

After teaching ten years at Sidwell Friends, I was granted a sabbatical for the 1983–84 school year. I enrolled in Buffalo State's Creative Studies graduate program for the fall semester, then spent the winter and spring terms at Pendle Hill, a Quaker center for study and contemplation outside of Philadelphia. The whole community there participated in one day-of-silence during the spring term. Over dinner, a student read aloud a passage in which the author taught a friend how to eat a tangerine. The friend

> popped a section of tangerine in his mouth and, before he had begun chewing it, had another slice ready to pop into his mouth again. He was hardly aware he was eating a tangerine. All I had to say was, "You ought to eat the tangerine section you've already taken."[9]

I was intrigued. The reading came from *The Miracle of Mindfulness* by Vietnamese Zen master Thich Nhat Hanh. I found a copy in the Pendle Hill bookstore and took it home where it lay unopened on the bookshelf. Three years later, Elisabeth, sick in bed, asked me to read to her. I took Thich Nhat Hanh's book from the shelf and began reading. Immediately, I was captured by his lesson on having unlimited time for oneself by seeing everything one does as for oneself. My students could benefit from hearing this too! I took the book to school and began reading it aloud for five minutes at the beginning of each math class. The students got it. When I finished the book, they asked for another and eagerly listened to its sequel, *The Sun My Heart*.[10]

Over the next years my life experienced a sea change. I started to meditate. Then, in 1989 I met Thich Nhat Hanh, "Thây" (pronounced "tie"), as his students call him, meaning "Teacher." I became one of his students and helped establish a practice community in his tradition in Washington, DC. After twelve years of active involvement in the Washington Mindfulness Community and participation in numerous retreats, I received an invitation in 2001 to come to Plum Village, Thây's monastery in southwest France, to receive transmission to become a teacher in his tradition.

I understood that the ceremony would include my offering an insight poem to Thây and his spiritual ancestors as well as receiving a personal poem from Thây. I felt intimidated. On occasion I'd been inspired to write a poem or two, none with the expectation that they'd contain special insight, much less that I'd have to read them aloud to Thich Nhat Hanh and the assembled Plum Village monastic and lay community. I couldn't see myself just sitting down and writing such a poem. My words would need to express an insight, and it would need to be about *something*. I wondered what that something could be. What was alive in me? What was my insight?

Ever since encountering the writing of Thomas Wolfe in high school, I'd been drawn to people who impressed me as free: Henry Miller, Ram Dass, the Grateful Dead, Thich Nhat Hanh. It would be wonderful to offer a vision of freedom in my poem, to find more freedom in writing it, and share this freedom with others, especially my students. I'd been reading alternative education texts and incorporating new methods into my math teaching. Yet true freedom in my personal life was rare. Unresolved issues dating back to childhood plagued me. I hoped to learn something fresh about freedom that would propel me on my path. Hoping to fertilize the soil of insight, I began discussing freedom with my friends. No sprouts appeared. Finally, a month before the transmission ceremony, I raised the question with Ted, my therapist. At the end of the session Ted wrote a few words on his pad and ripped it off saying, "Here's your assignment for next week, Richard." I looked down. On the first line he'd written "freedom from." Halfway down I saw the words "freedom to." I suppressed a sigh. Was this really going anywhere? During the following days I made entries in each category: *freedom from* and *freedom to*. I learned nothing. Disappointed, I reported my results to Ted at our next session. He just listened, taking in my disappointment.

A few days later, insight arrived. I awoke with a fresh understanding. Suddenly I saw that my knots—my negative habit patterns—were part of me. Untying them wasn't a prerequisite for freedom. This revelation translated itself into a poem which I respectfully offered to Thây and the ancestors during my transmission ceremony a few weeks later:

> This freedom – not freedom from,
>> from childhood habits,
>> from childhood fears;
>> not freedom to,
>> to open to the love enfolding me,
>> to know and live my truth.
> This freedom – freedom with,
>> with habits, with fears,
>> with heart protected,
>> truth hidden deep inside.
> This freedom – freedom with this moment,
>> just as it is.

This was the freedom I offered my math students when I invited them to tune into their thoughts and feelings before tests, to accept them but then to find that, whatever else their present moment held, it also held memories of past pride and success with mathematics. It was also the freedom these students had recording their thoughts and feelings, whatever they were, in the back of their journals confident of complete confidentiality. And it was freedom with their discomfort that I described in a contribution to Thich Nhat Hanh's and Katherine Weare's beautiful book on sharing Plum Village mindfulness practices with students *Happy Teachers Change the World*:

> When my students encounter obstacles, their first impulse is usually towards one of two extremes: they try to overcome them or they give up. The approach of welcoming obstacles, sitting with them, and seeing what gifts of understanding they have to offer is foreign to my students, yet it is one that could

serve them well in life. I ask myself how I can do a better job of modelling this way of relating to difficulties in the class-room. I realize I can begin by curbing my impulses to diagnose and suggest remedies for students' problems, and learn how to just be with the students and their problems.[11]

Another dimension of freedom had been important earlier in my life when my wife and I were choosing an elementary school for our daughter Shoshanna. She had thrived in a Waldorf[12] pre-school near us. With great anticipation, Elisabeth and I visited the Washington Waldorf School across town. I admired much of what we heard—their emphasis on stories and the arts, the opportunity students had to create their own textbooks, the absence of com-puters in the lower grades. I wondered: could their policy of keep-ing the same teacher with a class for eight years really work well for students? My biggest concern had to do with what seemed to be a lack of support for individual creativity and student empow-erment. Student was artwork displayed on the wall outside each classroom. One class exhibited drawings of trees, another draw-ings of dwellings. Art was prescribed for each age group. Teachers functioned as the window on the world for students, dictating les-sons students copied into the textbooks they created. There didn't seem to be any small-group work. Were there even class discus-sions? Did classroom communication consist primarily of lec-tures? Shoshanna was bright, imaginative, artistic, and creative. To me, this school's approach seemed limited. Fortunately, Elisabeth and I allowed ourselves plenty of time to make the decision. I vis-ited Sidwell Friends' Lower School and three other schools. From my perspective, none of the five schools felt right for Shoshanna. Elisabeth felt firmly that the Waldorf School was the right school. We held the question open and trusted guidance would come.

I was sitting in our Upper School Math Help Room one afternoon when a stranger poked his head through the door. He identified himself as Peter Morse, a teacher who in 1973 had left Sidwell Friends to teach high school math at the Washington Waldorf School. It was his place I took at Sidwell. Now he lived in Michigan, teaching the cycle of grades one through eight in another Waldorf school. Here was the perfect person to hear my concerns about Waldorf education.

"You describe Waldorf philosophy as 'education towards freedom'," I said to him. "How does that square with the fact that the students have so few choices?"

Peter responded,

> In a recent study in Germany comparing graduates of Waldorf schools with matched graduates of non-Waldorf schools, spouses, friends, colleagues, and bosses were interviewed. Among other things, the results showed that in the workplace, the person who questions the status quo is most likely a Waldorf graduate.

I responded by telling Peter about my time at Green Gulch Zen Center where I was introduced to meditation. "There, almost every minute was determined for me. I had no choices about schedule, work duties, even the food I ate. I didn't think about future decisions or judge those I'd already made. My mind was free to dwell on the present moment. I felt an internal liberty there that wasn't available when my life was top heavy with planning and critiquing."

Peter affirmed this. "As young children, Waldorf kids develop a sense of security, a sense of comfort in their world. They aren't overwhelmed by choices and uncertainties before they're ready. Later in their development," he added, "this gives them the confidence to take risks."

Indeed, it is the restrictive banks of a river that create its power and flow. Peter had convinced me. We applied to the Washington Waldorf School for Shoshanna's first grade experience.

Other family members also gave me opportunities to learn about freedom. During the last years of his life, my father became my most important teacher about radical freedom—freedom without regrets, without expectations, without fear. I wrote about this in:

Present Moment, Wonderful Moment

> When I was growing up, my father had so much to teach me—honesty, loyalty, generosity, attention to detail. Now, at age 79, he lives with Alzheimer's disease in a nearby nursing home and teaches me new lessons.

My father recognizes little of the past and makes no plans for the future. Spending time with him only works to the extent that I am able to participate in the present moment. Relieved of the necessity and possibility of conversation, I hold his hand, massage his neck, walk with him, and play with Shoshanna, now almost four years old. My father seems content to watch, with no need to join in the play.

To Dad, I am no longer anyone special. "Who is Richard Brady?" my father asks. Sometimes I am still his son, but often I am simply a visitor. Without expectations, I am allowed to be whoever Richard Brady is in the moment. But I have a much harder time accepting him, diminished as he is. When my father smiles and responds to me, fine. But when he naps through our visit or fumes out of all proportion when accidentally bumped, old angers surface and I wrestle with my need for him to be awake and polite.

He continually shows me my dependence on the past—my notion of home, for example. During his recent visit to our house, the two of us take a walk. Returning to the house, I say, "Let's go in. This is my home." "No!" he replies, "I don't know the people who live here." Luckily Shoshanna sees us through the window, opens the door and invites us in. Always a new person to my father, she is "wonderful," a child whose invitation he would never refuse. When we return to my father's nursing home, I do not tell him that this is his home. "Let's stop here," I say, "this looks like a nice place."

"Yes," he says.

My father lets go of feelings as easily as he lets go of knowing. One minute he enjoys a visit with us, and the next minute he is uncomfortable and ready to go. How can I accept these new inconsistencies? As I learn to be with my father however he is, I find that his trying feelings are just as subject to change as his pleasing ones. When he objects, I stop insisting that we've walked enough, and moments later Father is ready to take the shortcut back. In the same vein, no matter how slowly I drive, he wants me to slow down. We slow down, and he relaxes.

A few days after a recent visit to the nursing home, Elisabeth tells me she wishes I would sit and beam at her as I had at my father. How much easier to be completely present with a person minus the disruption of language, expectations, the past, and the future. "I'm learning how," I say.[13]

Certainly, language, expectations, the past, and the future also colored my perceptions of my students and theirs of me and of each other. All assumed new shapes as the students began working together in small groups in the late 1970s and my role increasingly became that of facilitator.

REFLECTIONS AND CONTEMPLATIONS

Contemplate an experience you've had of freedom.

What did you learn from it?

Psychologist Carl Rogers said, "The curious paradox is that when I accept myself just as I am, then I can change." What is your experience of this paradox?

What aspect of life is inviting your insight now?

LEARNING TOGETHER

My interest in student collaboration dates back to my University of Maryland summer course with Ron McKeen. One day he invited his friend Neil Davidson to teach the class. Similar to Ron's approach, Neil offered provocative questions: "Why do we always tell students what they need to know and never let them discover it for themselves?" He invited us to visit his summer school math class for elementary teachers. I was delighted. When I arrived, the class was divided into groups of four. They'd been studying parallel lines and were now researching parallelograms. Each group sought to discover why the opposite sides of these quadrilaterals had to be of equal length. To prove this, they introduced one of the parallelogram's diagonals and went on to prove that the two triangles thus formed were congruent. This proof is normally the province of the teacher or textbook, but these students were excitedly discovering the proof for themselves. A whole new chemistry of learning was rolling out before me. I felt privileged to watch and excited to be a teacher!

Small-group collaboration offered a compelling antidote to student competition. Observing it, I recalled how lonely I was as a student. In high school I'd missed out on true friendship. Now I wanted to dispense with my role of teacher-as-authority and become more like Mr. Landers, the nurturer, and like Ron, the facilitator. As a young teacher molded by a traditional math education and with traits modeled after my father's, I couldn't fathom how this might happen. But I was at the gate of the kingdom of synchronicity where my own openness, like the rays of the sun infusing a plant, produces fruit. I threw my energy into teaching. Beneath the surface of my consciousness, my brother's tragic life with brain damage had had a profound effect on me. I would never know how things might have turned out—how, for example, an alternative school might have served him. But now I had the opportunity to do all I could to promote the well-being of students under my care. I would be doing it in honor of my brother.

The innovative spirit of St. Mary's made it an ideal laboratory for testing unconventional ideas like student collaboration and discovery learning. It still took me a few years for favorable external conditions (readable texts and students interested in math) and internal conditions (my self-confidence) to manifest. During the late 1970s the cooperative education movement was beginning to pick up steam. More conferences, books, and approaches were available. I was inspired by a few books and attended several conferences, but my small-group pedagogy grew primarily from my own experience in the classroom.

In the beginning I assigned students to groups. I'd form new groups after each test with the intention that each student participate in a group with every other student sometime during the year. I also thought it wise to assign at least one of the more successful students to each group. Eventually, students in one of my classes complained they hadn't yet had opportunities to work with certain friends. They wondered if I was separating them on purpose. My assignment process was anything but transparent. I held my breath and told the students that one of them could draw the members of the next groups out of a hat. After that, each selection process proved to be a bit of high drama as names were drawn and groups composed. There were no more complaints.

Although I rarely received complaints from group members about how their groups were doing, it was apparent that some didn't function as well as others. A week or so after new groups formed, I'd give all the students index cards and ask them to let me know how their group was doing. When the students had journals, they'd respond to this query in the front for me to read. Whenever difficulties were reported, I'd meet with a group and tell them I understood there were some problems. Then I'd ask the group members to take a couple of minutes to reflect on what they might do to help resolve the problems.

Although my teaching approach was evolving, I rarely took time to reflect on it fully until Middle School Principal Harry Finks asked me to teach Math I to a group of eighth graders. I'd been teaching Math I to ninth graders and knew how challenging it was. The eighth graders would be very bright but unfamiliar with the rigor of an Upper School course. For guidance in letting them know what lay before them, I turned for advice to my ninth grade Math I students. How much should I reveal to the eighth graders about the course?

I ended up with seventeen pages of notes. "Whatever you give the eighth graders next year needs to be short and simple," Harry told me. Distilling my notes, I wrote *MATH I – AN INTRODUCTION*. This three-page summary set out my main goals, rationales, and methods. This wasn't theory; it was the product of experience. I was excited to be embarking on a new chapter of my life as a teacher.

MATH I – AN INTRODUCTION

In this introduction to Math I I would like to explain to you some of my main goals in this course, give you my reasons for them, and offer you an idea of how the course was designed to help you accomplish them.

TO BECOME A MORE INDEPENDENT LEARNER

As you progress through school and beyond, the focus of your learning experiences will be more and more on you. Eventually you will have the responsibility of determining how and where to find the knowledge you need and even that of determining exactly what knowledge you do need. One of the first steps in becoming a more effective independent learner is developing your ability to draw on sources of knowledge other than your teacher. In Math I you will have the opportunity to learn a great deal from your textbook and from your classmates. Much of your class time will be spent discussing and working on problems with other students. Your reading assignments will often cover material that has not been previously discussed in class. I will be on hand to help you clarify fuzzy areas and to help you get additional perspectives on what you have done.

TO USE YOUR LEARNING MORE EFFECTIVELY

You will be learning a lot in Math I and in your other courses. However, in the long run it will not be how much you learn that will determine the true value of your courses but to how much use you put that learning. Fortunately, many important kinds of learning (reading, studying, solving problems, working with others, and evaluating yourself more effectively) can be put to great use immediately. The usefulness of the mathematics you learn will largely depend upon how well you can make use of it in many different situations. For this reason, you will be presented with numerous opportunities to apply what you have studied in new and unfamiliar settings. Additionally, understanding why concepts are defined as they are and why methods work will begin to take on as much importance as learning the concepts and methods themselves.

TO BECOME MORE EFFECTIVE AT
HELPING OTHERS

The complexity of the problems encountered in all areas of human endeavor has increasingly called for the efforts of working teams and has multiplied communication between individuals. Different people bring to their work different strengths. For groups to function most effectively, it is vital that all members help one another make the most of their particular abilities. When this happens, all come away with much richer understanding and, invariably, better solutions to problems. During the year you will be a member of several small groups which will both review work done individually and work together on new material. This will involve a great deal of listening, questioning, explaining, and especially thinking about what will be said, is being said, and has been said.

TO BECOME MORE EFFECTIVE AT
SELF-EVALUATION

Whether they involve math concepts, problem-solving skills or aspects of learning in general, to make the most of your strong points and strengthen your weak areas, you need to be aware of what they are. Teachers can give you some valuable insights, but most of what they see are the end products of a long process. You are the only one in a position to see how you go about learning and applying your knowledge from beginning to end. To help you do this and make more effective use of what you find, you will be periodically answering a set of queries about how you handle different aspects of your work.

As you think about these goals, I hope that you too feel they are important ones. The course has been designed with them in mind. You'll probably find Math I different in many ways from other courses you have taken. One thing that will be familiar to you is the kind of math you'll be studying. We'll be spending most of the year on algebra, reviewing and extending many topics you've already studied, before investigating some important new ones later in the year.

These goals constituted far more than math skills. Indeed, they were keys to a fuller, more productive life. I felt grateful that as an educator and as a human being, I was beginning to inhabit what I was truly here to teach.

My two subsequent eighth-grade Math I classes received this same introduction. Coupled with the knowledge they wouldn't receive grades, all students came on board. Whether or not they continued in the honor's track the following year, all but the one mentioned previously appreciated the opportunity for the growth Math I provided them.

REFLECTIONS AND CONTEMPLATIONS

What goals for your students inform your teaching?

What goals do your students have that inform your teaching?

Recall a positive experience working on a team.

What conditions made it so positive?

Recall a challenging experience working on a team.

How did you respond to it? What did you learn from it?

ALONE NO LONGER

An old adage says we teach what we need to learn. This was true for me with regard to collaboration. I was teaching students to collaborate but had not been collaborating myself. Growing up, what I saw of collaboration was minimal. My parents' roles were well defined: My father supported the family and my mother cared for home and children. They were not unusual for their generation.

For years, my father ran a one-person business. Finally, he added a secretary. When he also added Jim, a young assistant about my age, Father treated him as he treated my brother and me. Jim received clear guidelines about how Father wanted him to do business. With incredibly high standards for himself and others, how would my father have worked with peers as colleagues? Similarly, I chose a profession in which I was in charge of my own classroom. I was free to innovate, handle homework in my own way, and create unique problems, projects, and units so long as I maintained academic standards and covered the mandated curriculum. I sometimes wondered what it would be like to teach with colleagues.

St. Mary's and David Mallery's seminars and workshops whetted my appetite for more ventures with like-minded instructors. Eventually in 1989 and again in 1990, I joined Joan Countryman, who had taught Problem Solving at St. Mary's in 1984, and her friend Arthur Powell to offer a four-day seminar on Creative Approaches to Secondary School Mathematics. I taught the *Group Investigation*[14] component.

Group Investigation, promoted by Israeli educators Yael and Shlomo Sharan, combines student-led learning with small-group learning. First, a class chooses topics that interest them within an area of inquiry. The students then form groups to study the particular topic that most appeals to them. For example, groups studying the civil rights movement might explore topics such as Dr. King, the Montgomery bus boycott, or related federal legislation. Each group then divides its topic among its members who compile their research and report to the class.

For the seminar, I chose a broad range of topics in advance and supplied literature on math-related areas, including problem solving, discovery learning, querying, evaluating, and integrating innovative strategies. After they perused the literature, participants divided into groups based on topics they wished to explore. Over the next several days, they used the *Group Investigation* model to research and report on their topic. It's rare for teachers to work with peers on a topic of common interest. What a pleasure it was to offer them *Group Investigation*. It dovetailed smoothly with Joan's focus on writing to learn mathematics and Arthur's focus on mathematical thinking. I was part of a team but had a distinct role. This would soon change.

After our second workshop, I looked up Neil Davidson, then president of the International Association for the Study of Cooperation in Education. Luckily, IASCE's next conference was scheduled in Baltimore. Neil invited me to submit a proposal to present a workshop. Most workshops focused on student collaboration, but I was more interested in models of faculty collaboration. Joan Countryman was happy to join me in offering *Exploring Staff Development Together*, a *Group Investigation* workshop focused on faculty collaboration. We'd work on creating and offering it together.

Six weeks prior to the conference Joan called to tell me she wouldn't be able to come. Unexpectedly, her daughter was getting married that same weekend. In a turmoil, I sought Neil's advice. "Call Linda Munger at Iowa State University," he suggested, "She attends our conferences and will definitely be interested in your topic." She was. Linda and I met for the first time the day before our workshop and planned how we'd work together. I was delighted by how smoothly our meeting went. Had I lucked out in finding a partner on the same wavelength?

The next day we began with our participants by explaining *Group Investigation* and handing out bibliographies divided into sections, including School Change and Improvement, Networking, Groups, Staff Development, and Leadership. Many books and articles lay out on two long tables. Our teachers divided into two groups and spent the next ninety minutes engrossed in exploring their topics. At the end, one of the four participants asked how many years Linda and I had worked together. This more than made up for the low attendance. Ten years passed before the conditions lined up for me to collaborate with another colleague again, this time co-leading mindfulness workshops for educators. During those years, I developed more ease and equanimity with the mystery that accompanies sharing control. I was more than repaid by the new ideas and different teaching styles contributed by my partners. Teaching together, we embodied the collaborative spirit we were inviting participants to share.

REFLECTIONS AND CONTEMPLATIONS

What teaching interest would you like to explore with other educators?

How can you initiate this?

Contemplate an experience you've had working with a colleague or a partner.

What did you learn from it?

TOGETHER WE ARE ONE

What was the life I was trying to prepare students for? Was it the life of the educated person my Westtown roommate James sought? Was it the life I was doing my best to live? Answers to this question grew in unexpected ways. One seed was planted in the late 1960s when I saw the film *Breathless* by French filmmaker Jean-Luc Godard. In it, a journalist asks a French philosopher, "What is your greatest ambition in life?" The philosopher answers, "To become immortal ... and then die." Over the years this phrase, "To become immortal ... and then die," returned to me again and again. I had no idea what it meant, but it seemed significant.

One Thursday morning in 1990, an algebra student approached me at the end of class to ask for help with a problem. It wasn't a complex method, and it was well explained in the text. I wanted my students to be autonomous, to learn how to solve problems themselves, and I was tempted to tell him so. Instead, I offered him the extra help he requested. Afterwards I went to Meeting for Worship where my thoughts turned to my mother. She was a fiercely independent woman. At age 77 she was still caring for my dad with Alzheimer's and my brain-damaged brother at home. When Elisabeth and I visited her, we'd urged her to get help. Mother steadfastly refused. As I sat in Meeting, I asked myself, did I want my students to end up like my mother? No. It was quite clear. I hoped they'd learn how much we need each other and how interdependent we are. Suddenly I saw that to reach that experience of interdependence, these teenagers needed first to find a sense of their own independence. The same was true for the philosopher in the Godard film. He needed to become aware of his immortality before being ready to let go of life.

Interdependence also came to mind when on a whim I asked students in one of my Sidwell math classes who the best teacher in the Upper School was. There was a long silence. Then two hands went up. The first student volunteered Fran Cleaver, our choral music director. The second agreed. Fran had a reputation for being a very demanding teacher. Her students sparkled in concerts and in school musicals. I assumed the students who put her name forward had this in mind, but I didn't ask for explanations. Eventually, I came to see more in their choice. Fran worked with ensembles. There were soloists, and, I imagine, hopes and disappointments in this respect. But Fran's focus was on helping students develop and use their abilities as contributions to a group performance—a significant responsibility taught in team sports as well but not in most of Sidwell's classrooms.

In my experience schools have been places where students are required to be responsible for their work and for their behavior. For most, that is about it. I encountered one exception in my explorations—Somerset School, a small alternative, independent high school in Northwest, Washington, DC. I'd heard from friends who knew it that it was truly a different kind of school, so I arranged to visit Somerset on one of my professional days. Their math classes looked very much like my own. Students came together to work in groups and pairs as the need arose, support as well as occasional explanation of new material was given by teachers.

As luck would have it, one of the regular meetings of all members of the school community occurred that day following classes. After students and faculty had settled into a large classroom, a senior began to chair the meeting by going over the agenda. As topics were introduced, hands were raised and a student recorded the names of those who wished to speak. All went smoothly until someone noticed that three students who'd been at school that day weren't present in the meeting. Another student volunteered to find them. He located the missing students in a nearby classroom and escorted them to the meeting. When an explanation for their absence was requested, a spokesperson for the group rose and addressed the community:

> Those of you whose parents pay for you to attend Somerset may take it for granted that everyone has the time to attend

this meeting. But the three of us have been working on math together because we need to complete it before going home. We have jobs to go to. We need to earn money to be able to attend this school.

There was silence. I was awestruck. The students had asked their community to understand interbeing at a deep level. They got up and left the room to resume their work.

This experience foreshadowed an occurrence many years later of a very different sort of absence. In 2010 Elisabeth and I were invited to be Friends in Residence at Pendle Hill. As we'd be living there, Walter Sullivan, then Pendle Hill's Dean, invited me to offer a weekend course. I'd loved the way Parker Palmer had used quotes, stories, and poems when I was his student at Pendle Hill twenty-six years earlier and had been inspired to start my own collection. This was the perfect time and place to offer a course in Parker's tradition. I could invite participants to contemplate their own lives through lenses provided by stories and poetry.

Mindful of physical challenges I was experiencing, Elisabeth wisely suggested I find someone to co-lead. I'd met Beth Popelka, a student in the Pendle Hill course I was taking, and immediately recognized her special gift for connecting and caring. Beth had formerly studied with Brazilian theater director Agusto Boal, founder of Theatre of the Oppressed. Boal was using stage experience to promote social and political change. Like her mentor, Beth's work was about breaking down barriers. When she spoke about it, I could see how she'd bring passion and dynamism to the weekend. I invited Beth to co-lead, and she accepted enthusiastically. Our Pendle Hill weekend course began to take shape.

Minding Our Lives: Looking Deeply at the Present Moment

Moments of challenge and opportunity are always present, yet we are not always aware of them. How do we recognize such a moment and receive its blessing? Participants will be introduced to mindfulness exercises that invite us to examine and embrace life, deepening our awareness of self and world. From this place of awareness, we will journal and share with others through word and gesture, blending the gifts of solitude and interconnection. We will offer our joy and suffering, fullness and emptiness. We will look at our troubles and our yearning. We will investigate mind, body, and spirit with an attitude of spacious acceptance, drawing on poetry and stories from a breadth of wisdom traditions.

Working with a partner, we took risks we wouldn't have taken alone. The largest was a role-playing exercise Beth led based on a powerful story by Rabbi Lawrence Kushner. In it several Nazi storm troopers board a bus looking for Jews. We chose the story because of its compelling altruism in the face of terror.

Stranger on the Bus

A light snow was falling and the streets were crowded with people. It was Munich in Nazi Germany. One of my rabbinic students, Shifra Penzias, told me her great-aunt, Sussie, had been riding a city bus home from work when SS storm troopers suddenly stopped the coach and began examining the identification papers of the passengers. Most were annoyed but a few were terrified. Jews were being told to leave the bus and get into a truck around the corner.

My student's great-aunt watched from her seat in the rear as the soldiers systematically worked their way down the aisle. She began to tremble, tears streaming down her face. When the man next to her noticed that she was crying, he politely asked her why.

"I don't have the papers you have. I am a Jew. They're going to take me."

The man exploded with disgust. He began to curse and scream at her. "You stupid bitch," he roared. "I can't stand being near you!"

The SS men asked what all the yelling was about.

"Damn her," the man shouted angrily. "My wife has forgotten her papers again! I'm so fed up. She always does this."

The soldiers laughed and moved on.

My student said that her great-aunt never saw the man again. She never even knew his name.[15]

First we read the story, then Beth divided us into two groups. One group re-enacted the story while the other witnessed. Next the groups switched parts as audience and actors. Finally, we offered the whole group a chance to journal and then share. When we first used it, the exercise evoked a moving response. When we repeated it at Pendle Hill the following year, the exercise brought up so much suffering in one participant that he left the room and refused to return. I felt my stomach tighten. What had this story touched in him? The group immediately stopped and sat in silence. Slowly we began to discern together what to do. One member, a third-grade teacher, spoke of children who were out of school because of personal or family problems: "Our class always composes a card expressing our sympathy, our love, and our hope that our friend will be back with us soon." Our group did precisely that. Someone delivered our homemade card to our missing comrade and he returned. Feeling grateful to be whole again, we welcomed him.

This experience, like the previous story of the absent students, could have provided a rich opportunity for reflection on what had just occurred. However, filled with relief, Beth and I went on to our next exercise, just as the Somerset community, doing what felt right for them, returned to the agenda item under consideration. Living without boundaries is seldom tidy. It offers profound lessons, but we need to stop to grasp them.

REFLECTIONS AND CONTEMPLATIONS

Contemplate a time when you chose to give up your independence in some way.

What feelings did you have before you did this? After you did it?

What did you learn about yourself?

NOTES

1 Godard, J. (Director) (1960). *Breathless*. Les Films Impéria; Les Productions Georges de Beauregard; Société Nouvelle de Cinématographie.

2 Rumi. (1995). "Two Kinds of Intelligence," in *The Essential Rumi*, trans. Coleman Barks with John Moyne, A.J. Arberry, and Reynold Nicholson. San Francisco: Harper San Francisco, 178.

3 Jacobs, H. (1970). *Mathematics, a human endeavor: A textbook for those who think they don't like the subject*. San Francisco: W.H. Freeman.

4 Postman, N. and Weingartner, C. (1969). *Teaching as a subversive activity*. New York: Delta.

5 Neill, A.S. (1960). *Summerhill: A radical approach to child rearing*. New York: Hart.

6 Freire, P. (1970). *Pedagogy of the oppressed*. New York: Herder and Herder.

7 Mailer, N. (1948). *The naked and the dead*. New York: Rinehart and Company.

8 Jay McTighe, Personal Communication, 1983.

9 Hanh, T.N. (1975). "Eating a tangerine," in *The miracle of mindfulness: A manual on meditation*. Boston: Beacon Press, 5.

10 Hanh, T.N. (1988). *The sun my heart: From mindfulness to insight contemplation*. Berkeley: Parallax Press.

11 Brady, R. in Hanh, T.N. and Weare, K. (2017). *Happy teachers change the world*. Berkeley: Parallax Press, 257.

12 For those interested in learning about Waldorf education, see: Wikipedia, "Waldorf education," accessed October 29, 2020, https://en.wikipedia.org/wiki/Waldorf_education.

13 Brady, R. "Present Moment, Wonderful Moment," *The Mindfulness Bell*, no. 5 (Autumn 1991): 30.

14 A good description of *Group Investigation* can be found in Yael Sharan and Shlomo Sharan, "Group Investigation Expands Cooperative Learning," *Educational Leadership* 47, no. 4 (Dec. 89/Jan. 90): 17–21.

15 Kushner, L. (1996). "Stranger on the Bus," in *Invisible Lines of Connection: Sacred Stories of the Ordinary*. Woodstock, VT: Jewish Lights, 81–82.

PART III

SEEING WITH THE HEART

To live is so startling it leaves little time for anything else.

—Emily Dickinson[1]

As Emily Dickinson asserts, when we stop to look and listen, startling connections with others, with our world, and with ourselves—with life—become possible. However, in a world where *more, faster, better* is the order of the day, there are few models for this kind of presence and seeing with the heart. I was fortunate to have teachers and friends who helped me stop, behold, and make deep connections, transcending the stories I told myself. From them I also learned how to share this dimension of *being* in my teaching. Because habits of *doing* were deeply ingrained in me, the support of groups and even of one other person were crucial for change to occur. The understanding of a situation, another person, or myself that came from a place of deep connection consistently informed my thoughts, words, and actions in profound ways.

For me Mary Oliver is the exemplar of one who sees with the heart. I've given her poem *The Summer Day* to many educators to contemplate, to journal on, and to share about with others.

The Summer Day

Who made the world?
Who made the swan, and the black bear?
Who made the grasshopper?
This grasshopper, I mean—
the one who has flung herself out of the grass,
the one who is eating sugar out of my hand,
who is moving her jaws back and forth instead of up and down—
who is gazing around with her enormous and complicated eyes.
Now she lifts her pale forearms and thoroughly washes her face.
Now she snaps her wings open, and floats away.
I don't know exactly what a prayer is.
I do know how to pay attention, how to fall down
into the grass, how to kneel down in the grass,
how to be idle and blessed, how to stroll through the fields,
which is what I have been doing all day.
Tell me, what else should I have done?
Doesn't everything die at last, and too soon?
Tell me, what is it you plan to do
with your one wild and precious life?[2]

Often young children have great curiosity and attention like Mary Oliver's. Somewhere along the way many lose this. At a weekly meeting, the student and faculty members of Sidwell's Spiritual Life Committee once shared about people in our lives who most inspired us. Family members, teachers, Gandhi, and Dr. King had already been mentioned when Samm, an eleventh grader, told us her greatest inspiration was herself as a five-year-old. She didn't elaborate. I wondered whether she was inspired by the way her five-year-old connected with life.

This same kind of wonder came to mind during a Plum Village mindfulness retreat some years later when my sharing group focused on the topic of looking deeply. Bob, a Protestant minister from Australia, pointed to a large spray of orchids in the center of the circle and described two ways of looking at them. On the surface, he could see the plant was a hybrid. Looking more closely, he could guess the varieties of orchids from which this one had sprung, emerging out of several generations of pure strains. On the other hand, Bob said, he could simply be with the flowers, feel their presence, and look at them just as they silently looked back at him. This second way of looking, like Rumi's second kind of intelligence, can get lost in the process of education.

"Engage in life with a sense of wonder." This was the message Sidney Parnes embodied. Sid, one of my most important teachers, was co-founder of Buffalo State's Creative Studies program. He was quiet, funny, brilliant, and passionate. I smile as I recall his book *The Magic of Your Mind*,[3] cartoons on every other page. One of the originators of Creative Problem Solving, Sid rubbed shoulders with just about everyone in the field of creativity. During the fall of my 1983–84 sabbatical, I was deeply nourished by an opportunity to study independently with Sid and to be a teaching assistant for his undergraduate course, *Applying Interdisciplinary Principles of Creative Behavior*.

This course in itself was remarkable. Each week he invited colleagues from diverse fields to talk about their work with creativity. Sid met regularly with his teaching assistants. At the beginning of the course he told us two things: "The structure is provided for students who need it. When you read their papers, keep the criticism positive with comments like, 'I find that it helps me to … You might try … and see what happens.' Only if you're unsatisfied, 'I'd like you to … and let me see it because….'" Sid read student papers after we'd written our comments on them. Once he pointed to a critical response I'd made:

"Do you understand what the student is saying here?" Sid asked.

"I have no idea," I replied.

"So rather than make a judgment about it, an appropriate response would be, 'I have no idea what you mean to say here.'"

What a teaching! How often do preconceived ideas make it difficult to hear what students have to say? Withholding judgment, we can welcome their deep looking and inner wisdom.

Some years ago Holy Cross University art history professor Joanna Ziegler shared a very different approach to nurturing these qualities. She related how she taught students the art of "beholding." The first week of her introductory course students were asked to meet in front of a piece of modern art at the local art museum. Most of these students, she told us, had never looked at modern art before and those who had weren't favorably impressed by it. Pointing to the picture before them, Professor Ziegler informed the students that writing about it would determine 20% of their course grade. "Your assignment," she said,

is to come to the museum once a week, sit, and look at this picture for twenty minutes, then go home and type a one-page paper telling me what happened for you during those twenty minutes. Each week's paper must be fresh. Use nothing from previous papers. It doesn't matter what happens. If you tell me, you will receive an A for that paper. Your reports must present your personal experience. Don't read anything about this picture, and, should a group come to view the picture and talk about it, depart.[4]

It was typical, Dr. Ziegler told us, for papers written the first few weeks to rant about the waste of time, the irrelevance of the assignment, and the absurdity of the picture. About the fourth week, students would begin to report observing things in the picture they hadn't previously seen. By the end of the course, students were describing it as "my picture." Professors who taught more advanced art history courses would tell Dr. Ziegler that her students were exceptional. They understood how to look at a painting.

REFLECTIONS AND CONTEMPLATIONS

Recall an experience of lingering and contemplating something—nature, a piece of art, a child.

Return to that experience and hang out there.

How does this feel? What does it teach you?

What do you plan to do with your one wild and precious life?

Contemplate a person you've known who embodies a sense of wonder.

What has this person contributed to your life?

BEHOLDING

"Beholding" is a cousin of discovery learning, the approach Neil Davidson adopted in his course for elementary school teachers and that I used in teaching Problem Solving at St. Mary's. It involves two things: giving students problems which are new to them and plenty of time for investigation. At Sidwell, I occasionally came up with an appropriate problem or question for my math students to use in this way. I'd invite students to take a few minutes to contemplate a problem or question for which they weren't prepared, then ask them to write in their journals, and, finally, to share in their groups.

These experiences were quite a contrast to the more usual classroom routine where students quickly identify the appropriate method to use, apply it, and go on to the next problem. This is a common approach to homework. This "fast learning," like "fast food," has limited nutritional value. Contemplative or "slow" learning is old-fashioned. It was the learning of medieval church schools and the monastery. It was characterized by "dwelling with" rather than studying and moving on. In this form of education, learners read a single passage several times, sit with it in silence, respond to it in a journal, and share responses to it out of the silence in pairs or with a group. Slow learning unites the learner and the learned just as eating meditation unites the diner and her food.

Just as slow foods have ingredients with high nutritional value, slow learning lends itself to particular kinds of textured experiences such as reading poetry, conducting investigations, addressing paradoxical, controversial and ambiguous material, and resolving challenging questions and problems. These kinds of experiences naturally generate slow learning. It was important to me to nurture habits of slow learning, particularly in students in too much of a hurry to get on to what was next. Ultimately, the habit of approaching learning and life in a mindful way has been for me the most important fruit of slow learning.

I began to devote the shortened, first math class of the year to the concrete task of raisin-eating meditation. I instructed students to take five minutes to eat three raisins with full awareness of their taste and texture, placing another one in the mouth only when no trace of the previous raisin remained. They weren't required to eat all three in the allotted time. It was a memorable way to start the year.

The next day I invited students to do their homework with the same concentration they'd given the raisins.

> Chew each homework problem thoroughly. Digest it fully before going on to the next. In that way you'll receive the full nourishment each problem has to offer. Even if you don't get to every problem, you'll come away with a better understanding of the material than if you hurry through just to get the job done.

With this permission, a student told me later, he felt free to give each problem the attention it warranted and not let the goal of completing all the assigned problems dictate his speed.

Early in the year I had a conversation with a student who wrote in her journal about the stress she'd experienced preparing for the first test. She related how thinking about the test had a negative effect on her studying. I wondered whether she was disturbed by thoughts about outcomes in all her activities. "Yes with one exception," she replied. Thoughts about how a scarf would turn out never intruded on her knitting. I suggested she experience studying for tests as another form of knitting, trusting that the "scarf" would turn out fine if she gave herself fully to her "knitting." This proved helpful to her.

During the school week, Sidwell's Meeting for Worship provided students a remarkable opportunity to look deeply, to behold their lives. Every Thursday morning our five hundred Upper

School students and faculty members gathered in silence. We sat together on bleachers in the gym for forty minutes. Occasionally, an inspired student or staff member would rise and share an insight—what Quakers call a message. My candid mentor, Head of School Earl Harrison, once said of Meeting's effect on students,

> It's like a live nerve that grows. You begin to get a sense of the fabric of imagination, of rest, of serenity, of "where will I be in the future?" If we can open up those questions during these essential, narcissistic, impressionistic years, that might take our graduates even further than a superior, formal education.[5]

During Meeting, there was ample time to reflect on issues I'd brought in with me, ones that arose inside me during Meeting, or ones prompted by the sharings of others. This wasn't always possible. Following a series of Meetings packed with student messages, I wrote the following article for *Horizon*, the Upper School newspaper.

Reflections from Meeting

I'm sitting in Meeting for Worship. I hear Cory recalling Monsieur Gueye saying, "If you don't know what you're looking for, you're not likely to find it." I think back on an experience two hours earlier:

I arrive in the Math Office and find an email from Varun waiting for me. It contains the URL of the Chaco Canyon "Magic Eye" picture he mentioned to me the day before. At first sight it's just a wall of red, grey and brown stones. I know there's a three-dimensional image hidden here, but have trouble seeing any sign of it. The reflection of the overhead light on the monitor is distracting. I turn out the lights and sit with eyes unfocused until I finally begin to see a small three-dimensional patch. Holding onto that piece of the image, I try to let the surrounding area come into alignment. One feature remains indistinct. As I move away from the image, the last section comes into sharp focus. Through an opening in the canyon wall, I'm viewing a rock formation and the canyon wall opposite. Amazing!

I had no idea what I was looking for, but I found it. In fact, when I think about the most important discoveries of my life—my wife, my spiritual path, Sidwell Friends—never did I know what I was looking for.

Meeting for Worship: When I arrive, I seldom know what I'm looking for. I'm often as surprised by the insights that arise in me as those coming in response to others' messages. Yes, occasionally I come to Meeting with a problem I want to think through. It may occupy my mind for most of Meeting, and I may find a resolution. But seldom is this a true insight. Epiphanies are more likely to show up when I'm able to stop thinking about a solution and simply sit—"hold it in the Light," as Friends say. This process is a lot like seeing the third dimension in a Magic Eye picture. I can't figure it out. No one else can show it to me. I must be patient and let it arrive. I can't make it happen; I can only let it happen.

In my classroom I post a Magic Eye Picture of the Week. When I get to class, students are invariably clustered around it. Some have looked at similar pictures for years, never discovering the hidden image, yet, drawn by the challenge and mystery, they keep coming back to look at new ones.

There is challenge and mystery in finding something of value in Meeting. I've often heard students say they get more from Meeting as they grow older. I wonder about this. Do they grow more patient? Make more of an effort to eliminate distracting thoughts by quieting and centering? Do they become more attentive to what they could not have predicted? Perhaps Meeting has become a refuge for them, a place to de-stress, to quell all the thinking and truly rest. Occasionally this happens to me. At the end of Meeting I feel as though my mind has been bathed.

I yearn for more such Meetings with you. And I'm moved by so many of your messages. I like taking these messages to a place of inner stillness and sitting with them for a while, dwelling with them. This year in Meeting, with too little space or silence between so many wonderful messages, I find it difficult to locate that place of mystery.[6]

Learning to sit in Meeting itself was pretty much discovery learning. There were relatively few Quaker students or faculty members. Most of us had to figure out for ourselves how to relate to these weekly times of gathering in silence. A few years after my arrival at Sidwell, student interest in Meeting for Worship waned. Students began whispering during Meeting and otherwise disrupting the worship. In an effort to salvage the Meeting, the faculty discontinued all-school Meetings and instituted smaller, more intimate gatherings. Each was centered around a particular theme. These Centered Meetings, as they were called, were led by faculty and/or students. Centered Meetings alternated with small Meetings for Worship.

Wanting to share my passion for jazz, I decided to offer a Centered Meeting using the Smithsonian's collection of jazz recordings. I hoped our experience of shared listening would support Meeting for Worship, complementing the inward listening we did there. I was bewildered when a number of students were unable to focus. They fiddled or found some distraction. Did the jazz I invited students to listen to evoke responses like those of Dr. Ziegler's students to their modern art painting? I didn't know. It never occurred to me to play the same jazz piece every time we met.

Maybe the students hadn't learned how to listen to music, or was it jazz itself with its improvisational nature? Many years later I was privileged to attend a weekend on music, meditation, and mindfulness at Kripalu Yoga Center. There, Kripalu's Larissa Hall Carlson amplified our awareness through breath and body practices and Boston Symphony Orchestra's Marc Mandel helped us listen to and understand recordings of musical pieces we later heard played live by the Boston Symphony Orchestra across the road at Tanglewood. I suspect that a little mindful movement might have helped my jazz listeners too, just as it did my algebra students later on.

The practice of simply listening to sounds might have been a good place to start with my jazz group. Lisa Flook, a research scientist at the Center for Investigating Healthy Minds at the University of Wisconsin-Madison, once shared a mindfulness practice, which is a favorite with preschoolers. Asking us to raise both hands, she sounded a chime. We were instructed to keep our hands raised until we could no longer hear the chime, then lower them to our abdomens and breathe in and out three times. I used this practice in working with teachers, but asked them to continue to listen to whatever sounds were present even after lowering their hands. Giving one's full attention to the chime is relatively easy. However, when listening to whatever sounds are present, people frequently begin thinking about the sounds they're hearing, naming their sources, wondering about them, making associations, and wandering off in other directions. Even more challenging is being fully present to another person.

REFLECTIONS AND CONTEMPLATIONS

Contemplate an experience of slow learning in your teaching.

In your life as a student.

Where did these experiences lead?

Recall a time you found something you weren't looking for.

How did that come about? What did you learn from the experience?

How did you learn to listen?

PRESENCE

Being present to others can be nurtured in simple ways. When it comes to teaching interpersonal mindfulness to young people, mindfulness educator Susan Kaiser Greenland is my inspiration. At a Mindfulness in Education Network conference, Susan once showed a video of a third-grade class sitting on the floor in a circle. Each child in turn looked at the child on his or her left and said something like, "Hello, Bill, your eyes look brown." The feeling of connection that moved around the circle was palpable.

Being present to another can be profound. This was so for me in 1992 during an outdoor walking meditation in Plum Village, Thich Nhat Hanh's community in southwest France. It was usual to stop for a short period of sitting or mindful exercise. However, one day, the leader asked each of us to silently find a partner. As we stood with our companions, he asked us to look at our own hands.

> These hands have been with you since before your birth. They've served you your entire life. The story of your days and years, your joys, your sorrows—all of these are present in your hands.

Following directions, my partner offered me one of her hands. I held it tenderly in mine. For three long minutes with no words, with no thoughts, I gently sensed what this hand was telling me about her life. Then we switched roles. She studied my hand. We'd come together as strangers. Suddenly we knew each other in a way no other living being did. The profundity and uniqueness of this experience, along with its silent context, made it easy for me to focus completely on my partner. For me, listening with total attention to another person speaking is much more challenging.

Twice during an eight-day retreat for Italian teachers I invited half the group just to listen for four minutes to their partners sharing anything they wished to about their experiences of reading and responding to a poem. The listeners were asked not to comment, not to ask questions or say anything, and not to express nonverbal approval or disapproval. Listeners usually find these instructions difficult to follow. Whether their experiences are similar to or very different from their partner's, many find it hard to contain their reactions. They're not just listening to their partner. They're thinking about what they're hearing, comparing it to their own experience, often appreciating some aspect of it, occasionally having some kind of negative response. Because they're not just listening, but also having personal responses, their positive and negative judgments are hard to contain. In addition, because they're filtering what they're hearing through their judgment, they may not be hearing well exactly what's being said.

During the retreat in Italy I was paired with a participant on the first occasion. Observing the second time, listeners appeared remarkably attentive, yet they remained inexpressive. Afterwards, on inviting participants to describe their listening experience to the whole group, I was disappointed when no one volunteered. Then Loredana, a teacher in a school for teenagers in Palermo, shared that she'd found "just" listening a big challenge. She had done her best to practice it as she listened and, for a brief moment, something completely unexpected happened. As she listened, she seemed to vanish. There was no longer a separation between her partner and herself. It was as if she were hearing her partner's words from inside the other woman. Later Loredana told me she'd had similar experiences of going "beneath the words" when listening to her son. At her school she had a reputation of being a good listener to students and parents, but it wasn't this "just" listening. She supposed that others, like herself, were constantly preparing responses as they listened. This time, knowing no response was expected of her, she felt free. She was able to stop thinking and simply listen. Loredana felt changed. It was now clear to her that it was possible to listen deeply to a relative stranger. She pledged to take this practice into her life as a parent, friend, and teacher, inspiring all of us to "just" listen to the others in our lives.

How we listen and respond to others is intimately connected to how we listen to ourselves. This quote, often attributed to psychiatrist Viktor Frankl, speaks volumes:

> Between stimulus and response there is a space. In that space is our power to choose our response. In our response lies our growth and our freedom.[7]

When another person says something that upsets us, the space referred to above may be almost nonexistent we react so automatically. Whether our reaction is directed at the other person or is strictly internal, in that moment we're aware of no other possible reaction. This reality is the focus of a practice called "The Four Chairs"[8] which I learned from Nonviolent Communication trainer Peggy Smith, a practice I shared with several groups of Italian teachers.

Acknowledging the challenging interactions the teachers faced at school and at home, I asked them to recall an incident when another person had said something that upset them and to write down the words the person uttered. Then I sat in the first of four chairs in the front and listened as a volunteer, now playing the role of the person who upset her, directed the disturbing words she'd heard at me. Playing the volunteer's role, I reacted to these words belligerently but explained that this response may have been internal, not voiced. I moved to the second chair, and the volunteer again directed the disturbing words at me. This time, again playing the volunteer's part, I took self-blame for whatever I had provoked in the other person. Moving to the third chair, I reflected on the feelings that I had on hearing the upsetting words and the universal human needs[9] from which these feelings arose, giving myself empathy. Finally, in the fourth chair, I became curious about the feelings and needs that might have been behind the other person's upsetting words and made an empathic guess.

The point of this exercise isn't that any one of these responses is "correct," but that four very different ways of receiving someone's upsetting words are possible. If the receiver is aware of these choices and has cultivated the space Frankl refers to, it is possible for her to choose her response. With this understanding, the other participants in the teacher groups reflected on the words that had upset them and formulated responses which related to each of the four chairs.

Using myself as an example—because others' anger was a problem for me growing up, I would automatically sit in chair 2 and experience self-blame or shame, my upset with the provocateur hidden safely from my own sight. After getting in touch with my anger later in life, I often found myself reacting from chair 1, responding irritably or departing with my aggravation unexpressed. In time, my mindfulness practice offered me space to be more aware of my feelings and move from chair 1 or 2 to chair 3. There, reflection often revealed that my feelings had as much to do with childhood experiences as with current ones.

My experience with chair 4 has been the most complex. Later in this book I describe an occasion when I responded immediately to anger with compassion for the other person. It occurred in Plum Village, where I felt peaceful, relaxed, and suffused with the positive energy of mindfulness. On other occasions it was likely that I had bypassed my own hurt when I immediately sat in chair 4. Taking care of others but ignoring one's own wounds is endemic in the helping professions. There is wisdom in airline crew members' instructions to passengers to put their own oxygen mask on first.

"The Four Chairs" is an excellent exercise to help participants become aware of different responses to upsetting situations and try them out. Often our responses are habitual and, in the throes of confrontation, we may not get beyond them. Even so, later on we might become aware of the chair we sat on and may still be sitting on, then decide to move to a different one. "Getting up" and "moving" in the midst of an encounter becomes more possible as the space between stimulus and response increases. This has been one of the most important results of my own mindfulness practice.

REFLECTIONS AND CONTEMPLATIONS

Recall an experience of connecting with another person in silence.

Recall an experience of just listening to another person. Of just being listened to?

What emotions did you feel then or feel now as you recall these experiences?

Reflect on disturbing words someone said to you and your possible response from each of the four chairs.

Which response feels right? Why?

STOPPING

Being fully present to anything, whether it's people, art, music, mathematics, or oneself, requires stopping first. Once Ann, an experienced Sidwell teacher, and I were leaving a first meeting for new teachers where I'd cautioned them to monitor the number of extra duty assignments they took on. From my experience, I'd told them, the first year of teaching at Sidwell Friends had a steep learning curve. Ann remarked to me that even without taking on any extra responsibilities, life at school was already too full. I agreed and made a suggestion which I hoped might be helpful to both of us. "Every time we see each other this year, no matter where we are and what we're doing, let's stop, smile to each other, and breathe slowly in and out three times." Ann was not a meditator and wasn't familiar with mindfulness practice. Still, this idea appealed to her. We honored our agreement for the entire year. Stopping and smiling helped us both be more present to the sacred work of teaching. Eventually Ann became curious about how the idea of doing this practice had come to me. I told her about my mindfulness experience and about using bells of mindfulness as invitations to stop and come back to the present moment during retreats—any kinds of bells, including telephone bells and clock chimes. "We're human bells of mindfulness for each other," I told her. Ann connected with this. She began to explore, attending days of mindfulness and mindfulness retreats by herself and with family members.

There are many ways to promote stopping and being present. I once heard a professor describe the very different way he started his classes. Having been deeply affected by Thây's slow, graceful manner of erasing whiteboards during his talks, the professor began his lectures in a similar fashion. The message was clear: "We're here to pay attention to everything." His students got it. So did he.

Many students and teachers have not encountered anyone who embodied stopping and being present. Anh-Huong, a niece of Thich Nhat Hanh's, raised this awareness when she came as a guest to a twelfth-grade Conflict Resolution seminar I was fortunate enough to offer at Sidwell. Anh-Huong spoke to us about how to develop inner quiet. She pointed out that inner turmoil which can elicit feelings of anger, shame, desire, and fear is most often rooted in thinking about the past or the future. The antidote Anh-Huong offered is to return to the present moment, to the here and now, using breathing as our anchor. She then shared a practice with us:

> Breathing in – I have arrived.
> Breathing out – I am home,
> Breathing in – in the here,
> Breathing out – in the now.

"In the present moment," she told us, "we can find more than enough conditions for peace and happiness." After Anh-Huong left, one student remarked, "For years, people have been telling me the things we just heard. This is the first time I've met someone who lives them." Indeed, Anh-Huong's teachings were not only in her words, but in her spacious and relaxed presence. Like Anh-Huong, my ability to be present had benefitted from practicing mindfulness.

REFLECTIONS AND CONTEMPLATIONS

Contemplate an experience of stopping during your workday. Stopping at home.

Where did these experiences lead?

Contemplate a person you've met who for you embodies inner peace.

What did you learn from this person?

DISCOVERING MYSELF

I'd changed a great deal during my thirty-four years of teaching at Sidwell Friends. In the spring of 2007, with my retirement approaching, I decided to reflect on my goals as a teacher. My principal, Jeff Guckert, gave me an extra incentive by inviting me to bid farewell to the departing seniors at an Upper School collection the day before graduation. I began this assembly with a few words from education writer William Glasser:

"There are only two places in the world where time takes precedence over the job to be done. School and prison."

This led me to the question, "What's the job to be done?" I shared the answer I had found several years before in *Parent/Teen Breakthrough: The Relationship Approach*[10] by Mira Kirshenbaum and Charles Foster. They say, "Teens have only two jobs to do: to figure out who they are and to leave home."

After a pause I continued, "During my thirty-four years at Sidwell Friends, I've worked with a number of self-confident people, and I've been inspired to look at and have faith in myself. However long you've been at our school, I hope you too have found models, people you wish to emulate." I went on to reflect on the more than one thousand Meetings for Worship I'd attended during my years at Sidwell, hours that had played a vital role in coming to know myself.

Were you able to learn faster than I did? As for leaving home, home is ideally a place where unconditional love is bestowed in full measure. How wonderful if all of you go on to places where you receive unconditional love. Sidwell Friends tries to help you make a home inside yourself. In Meeting for Worship, you've stood before five hundred peers and faculty members and apologized to friends, shared losses and fears without embarrassment or excuse, revealing to all of us the power of self-acceptance and love.

"In its celebration of uncommon excellence Sidwell Friends falls short as a home," I said, going on to relate words of Jim Matlack, a Quaker speaker, at a meeting of Sidwell faculty and parents. "The radical message of George Fox, founder of Quakerism, that there is that of God in every person," Matlack said, "poses a profound challenge to Friends Schools. It implies that differences related to academic, artistic, and athletic achievement pale in comparison to the sacred nature all humans have in common."

"Striving for uncommon excellence," I continued, "whether we're students or teachers, challenges our acceptance and love of ourselves as we are, our ability to inhabit our true home." I observed Sidwell Friends making progress. "This collection is able to take place the day before graduation, but in prior years this day was devoted to an awards assembly where only a small number of seniors were celebrated. Today we celebrate all of you. Every one of you is holy, worthy of celebration. I'm proud to be retiring from a school that no longer gives awards. I wish we no longer gave grades."

I concluded with a short meditation:

Breathing in, I am aware of myself.
Breathing out, I am home.

It would have been difficult to recognize the Richard who began teaching at Sidwell Friends thirty-four years earlier in the Richard who spoke that morning.

During my sabbatical twenty-four years earlier, my time as a student at Pendle Hill first provided me many opportunities to reflect on who I was becoming. My greatest insight surprised me during a course on Quaker journals. Each student read and reported on two journals, one written between 1650 and 1800 and the other written after 1800. The earlier journal I choose was written by Sarah Grubb, an English Quaker who lived from 1756 to 1790. I was drawn to her in part because she was a teacher. As I read her journal, I copied passages such as the following onto 3x5 cards:

> As to the performance of great works, I look not for it; my mind is taught to believe that I have no right thereto, or reason to expect that an instrument so feeble as myself, and so little a time in use, is likely to be owned, in any extraordinary degree, in the discharge of my small part of the great work. But my spirit hath often been dipped into sympathy inexpressible, with a seed in those parts, of which I have not yet attained outward discovery...[11]

I might have written these words myself about my hope to make changes in the traditional educational culture of Sidwell Friends. Although Sarah Grubb lived about 300 years ago, she was familiar to me. I had a sudden epiphany. She and I were both the "introverted, intuitive, thinking, judging" (INTJ) Myers-Briggs personality type. The Myers-Briggs Type Indicator, based on the work of Carl Jung, describes INTJ individuals as *independent, strategic, logical, reserved, insightful, and driven by their own original ideas to achieve improvements.*[12] It seemed to me that Sarah and I experienced life in a similar way. I devoted ample time to studying this journal of my new-found sister. I wanted to deepen my recognition of her and, in so doing, of myself.

Sarah was a person of deep faith who subjugated her own will to guidance from Spirit. Though Sarah received divine instructions throughout her life, the thought that my own inner guide might be grounded in Spirit never crossed my mind. I was routinely directed by will, not obedience. I wasn't prepared for Sarah's level of commitment to a full flowering of the spiritual life.

The clues that something was missing were there, but I didn't recognize them. Principals appreciated what my students were learning in my math classes, but suggested that my teaching might be more inspired. They didn't seem to appreciate my teaching style as facilitator, and I wondered if they understood the premises behind small-group learning. Eventually I came to see that I lacked a passion for mathematics. My passion was for growth. Math was the vehicle. This started to become clear five years after my time at Pendle Hill when I met Thich Nhat Hanh and made a commitment to practice mindfulness. Another twelve years passed before I began using mindfulness in teaching stress reduction to ninth graders. Mindfulness, not mathematics, was the true treasure I wanted to share with students.

During my last two years of teaching mathematics, when I'd added an opening period of contemplative practice to the ongoing small-group learning in my classes, an administrator happened to observe one of my tenth-grade classes. Afterwards, she told me how impressed she was with the quality of the group discussion of math problems. She connected this with the unhurried pace and focus of the class established by the opening period of silence, reading, and journal writing. Her observations were amplified by a student writing at the end of the year.

> I will cherish every day's fun conversation and banter, for I learned much, even when off topic. It was immensely enjoyable and by far my favorite class. The atmosphere was just the way it should be, an optimum learning environment.

REFLECTIONS AND CONTEMPLATIONS

Contemplate an experience that helped you discover who you are.

What did you learn from it?

Recall what it was like to leave home.

What internal and external conditions facilitated this?

Have you had the experience of encountering yourself in someone else? What did you learn?

DEEP COMMUNITY

A fairly solitary student myself and again as a teacher, I was always on the lookout for ways to foster community. Introducing small-group learning into my math classes and collaboration into my workshops and retreats provided opportunities for me to learn about and experience community as well, eventually expanding my notion of community beyond any bounds I'd imagined.

Student group work had its problems. From its beginning in my classes in the late 1970s, some students complained about others who showed up without having completed their homework. The unprepared students asked questions but contributed little. To solve this, my initial idea was to begin counting homework as part of semester grades. I was still pondering this option in 1981 when I attended my first Creative Problem Solving Institute in Buffalo. This annual weeklong gathering of inventors, artists, educators, consultants, business people, and helping professionals was my introduction to Sid Parnes, one of its creators. The spirit of collegiality was so alive there that I, usually shy, felt open to seeking advice from others.

At CPSI I asked Bill Mitchell, a management trainer with IBM, about small-group responsibility. He suggested each small group designate a leader who checked to see that everyone had done the homework. I could choose group leaders or allow each group to select their own, then explicitly turn the leadership over to them. "After all," Bill said, "you can see this as a group problem rather than one between you and the group." I was intrigued by this fresh way of looking at the power dynamic.

In his plenary talk the next evening, creativity expert Oz Swallow told us, "You can't hold others responsible for their actions. You can only hold them accountable. Responsibility arises from within. It can't be taught. All you can do is create situations in which a person can choose to be responsible." The next day I noticed him in conversation with a woman I didn't know. I waited to see if Oz would entertain a question from me. Their chat ended, and the woman, Marcy, a management consultant, addressed me directly, inviting connection. "What's on your mind?" she asked. I outlined my problem, my initial idea, and Bill's advice.

"Don't count the homework," Marcy advised, "They're already doing worse on tests because they haven't done their homework thoroughly." Then, echoing Oz, she added, "You can't teach responsible behavior. It has to come from within."

Wondering how I could better support the small groups, I responded, "Maybe I should explain why groups are important and let students know that if they can't make a commitment to a group, they shouldn't be part of it."

"No," Marcy replied, "You want everyone to participate in a group. This key element of your course is just as true outside the classroom. Students need to learn how to support one another. The business model builds in accountability through a group leader because their bottom line is results. If, as part of a team, people grow and become more responsible, that's a plus."

This was all I needed to hear. It was what I'd come to CPSI for—a fresh kind of exchange that nourished me as a learner. The following fall I divided all my math students into groups and introduced the homework process this way:

> Occasionally, some of you won't have enough time to complete your homework. When you see this is likely, try to complete the reading and work on a variety of problems so you'll be able to participate fully in your group. If you're not able to do this, you'll be a drag on your group. Please tell them you need to take some time in the Math Help Room to work on your own before joining them. We all understand that situations come up from time to time that get in the way of homework. This will only be a problem if it becomes a habit.

The idea that students spent most of their time in class working with others was considered radical. I'd pledged to make it work and did everything I could to support it. At the end of each unit, before the students moved on to new groups, I asked them to write notes to all the members of their current group thanking them for their contributions. I discovered how important this was to the students when I once forgot to provide for the note writing and was immediately reminded by the class.

In his June 1992 Plum Village retreat, I received a prize lesson about collaboration from Thây, who then had been my teacher for three years. Before inviting us to leave the meditation hall for our first outdoor walking meditation of the retreat, he asked us to be aware of others walking nearby. "You may notice someone walking very beautifully. If so, there's no need to be jealous. That person's practice is supporting your own. Similarly, your walking practice supports the practice of others around you." He then gave each of us a sticker to put in one of our walking shoes: *I walk for you*. Seeing the sticker each day as I slipped on my shoes for walking meditation, I felt myself one with my fellow retreatants.

Later that summer, before school began, I ordered a thousand stickers reading: *I learn for you*. When I introduced small-group work the first day of class, I handed out the stickers, They went on the covers of textbooks—a reminder, I told them, that their learning was also for the benefit of other students, and vice versa. In Thich Nhat Hanh's tradition, practicing mindfulness in a *sangha*, or spiritual community, is of prime importance. To give and receive support makes the *sangha* or the classroom a home for all.

Collaboration and community building were themes in my work with teachers and other adults as well. In the Minding Our Lives course Beth and I taught at Pendle Hill, we envisioned starting with introductions that might begin to build heartfelt community. We were certain that the unique resources brought by each of our adult students would enrich the course. We used a favorite story from Rachel Naomi Remen's book, *My Grandfather's Blessings*, which had jolted my own worldview of teachers. I came to see this story as a cornerstone of cooperative learning. Beth and I began our weekend reading it aloud to our participants:

Teachers Everywhere

I can clearly remember something that happened when I was in third grade. I was walking with my mother on a downtown street in New York City, pushing through crowds on our way to I no longer remember where. I had just been put into a special class at school because I had done well on an IQ test, and my new teacher had told us that being in her class meant that we were brighter than most of the people in the country. As we moved through the hurrying crowds, I remembered this and was filled with an eight-year-old's outrageous pride. I told my mother that my teacher had said that I was smarter than most of the people around us. She stopped walking immediately and knelt down so that we were at eye level with each other. As the crowd flowed past us on either side, she told me that every one of the people around us had a secret wisdom; each of them knew something more about how to live, about being happy, about loving than I did.

I looked up at the people passing by. They were all adults. "Is this because they are all grown-ups, Mama?" I asked her, taken aback. "No, darling. It will always be that way," she told me. "It is how things are." I looked again at the crowd moving around us. Suddenly I wanted to know them all, to learn from them, to be friends.

This lesson became lost among the many others of my childhood, but shortly after I became a physician, I had a dream that was so powerful that I remembered it even though I did not understand it. In this dream, I am standing in the threshold of a door. I seem to have been standing there a long time. People are passing through the door. I cannot see where they are going or where they have come from, but somehow this does not seem to matter. I meet them one at a time in the doorway. As they pass through they stop and look into my face for a moment and hand me something, each one something different. They say, "Here, here is something for you to keep." And then they go on. I feel enormously grateful.

Perhaps we are all standing in such a doorway. Some people pass through it on their way to the rest of their lives, lives that we may never know or see. Others pass through it to their deaths and the Unknown. Everyone leaves something behind. When I awoke from that dream, I had a sense of the value of every life.[13]

As we finished reading, we asked students to write about gifts they'd received from animate and inanimate teachers. After we all wrote in our journals for a few minutes, I pointed out that the gifts we'd written about were offerings we brought with us to the course. "Take a few minutes to choose one gift you'd like to share," I said. "Then create a gesture that embodies that gift." As an example, I bent over in laughter, a gesture for the gift of humor I'd be offering. To close the session, we stood in a circle for introductions. One by one, we first shared names and where we came from. Then, turning to the person next to us and striking our gesture, we said, "and the gift I'm bringing to offer this weekend is…, and named it with our bodies and our words." The introductions and offerings proceeded slowly around the room. One person shared the gift of listening, cupping an ear. Another shared creativity with arms and palms extended. A third offered the gift of tears, fingers caressing her cheeks. By the time the circle was complete, a rich sense of intimacy infused the room. We could all feel it.

Toward the end of the weekend, after several opportunities for personal reflection, we returned to the whole group, to focus on Thich Nhat Hanh's teaching on "interbeing," a term he coined. We used his poem, *Please Call Me by My True Names*. He wrote it after receiving news of a 12-year-old Vietnamese girl jumping into the Gulf of Siam after a sea pirate raped her. Years before, when I first read this poem, it evoked wonder but not recognition. I grew up seeing the world composed of distinct entities. I began to understand the poem more deeply when Thây recited it aloud. Thây transmits his teaching at levels that transcend the intellectual, beyond words and notions. My own connection to others began to expand.

My understanding of interbeing flowered in other ways as well. Mindfulness practice helped loosen my sense of separateness. At a heart level, I was more open, connecting, and empathic, but I couldn't hope to teach interbeing as Thây had. I'd come to know interbeing; he embodied it. On our teaching weekend, Beth and I wanted to offer a taste of interbeing, a feeling of it, not just an idea. We decided to use Thây's poem:

Please Call Me by My True Names

Do not say that I'll depart tomorrow
because even today I still arrive.

Look deeply: I arrive in every second
to be a bud on a spring branch,
to be a tiny bird, with wings still fragile,
learning to sing in my new nest,
to be a caterpillar in the heart of a flower,
to be a jewel hiding itself in a stone.

I still arrive, in order to laugh and to cry,
in order to fear and to hope.
The rhythm of my heart is the birth and
death of all that are alive.

I am the mayfly metamorphosing on the surface of the river,
and I am the bird which, when spring comes, arrives in time
to eat the mayfly.

I am the frog swimming happily in the clear pond,
and I am also the grass-snake who, approaching in silence,
feeds itself on the frog.

I am the child in Uganda, all skin and bones,
my legs as thin as bamboo sticks,
and I am the arms merchant, selling deadly weapons to
Uganda.

I am the twelve-year-old girl, refugee on a small boat,
who throws herself into the ocean after being raped by a sea
pirate,
and I am the pirate, my heart not yet capable of seeing and
loving.

I am a member of the politburo, with plenty of power in my
hands,
and I am the man who has to pay his "debt of blood" to my

people,
dying slowly in a forced labor camp.

My joy is like spring, so warm it makes flowers bloom in all
walks of life.
My pain is like a river of tears, so vast it fills the four oceans.

Please call me by my true names,
so I can hear all my cries and laughter at once,
so I can see that my joy and pain are one.

Please call me by my true names,
so I can wake up,
and so the door of my heart can be left open,
the door of compassion.[14]

Beth divided a copy of the poem into parts, numbered the parts,
cut them into strips, and placed them around a small table. I read
the poem aloud. Each student selected from the table a strip of
paper containing a few lines of the poem, then developed a gesture to illustrate those lines. Sitting in a circle, participants rose
in numerical order, read the part of the poem they'd picked and,
still standing, offered their gestures—a bird tentatively flapping
wings, a young girl preparing to jump into the sea. By the end of
our sharings, the poem had come to life, visible in and to all of us.
Finally, we wrote in our journals, each of us processing the poem
on our own.

This poem challenged both my tendency to judge people as
good or bad and my habit of identifying only with the good.
I thought of growing up in the shadow of my father's judgment. Some of his business associates were pleasant, others dis-
agreeable, some honest, others dishonest. Dichotomies were part
of his understanding of life. Mine as well. I think of Aleksandr
Solzhenitsyn's words:

> If only there were evil people somewhere insidiously com-
> mitting evil deeds, and it were necessary only to separate them
> from the rest of us and destroy them. But the line dividing
> good and evil cuts through the heart of every human being.
> And who is willing to destroy a piece of his own heart?[15]

REFLECTIONS AND CONTEMPLATIONS

Recall an experience of being deeply interconnected, of "inter-being" with others.

Reflect on its effect on you.

Recall an experience you've had with cooperative learning as a student. As a teacher.

What elements of these experiences were important to you?

What are the most important gifts you've received from others? That you have to give to others?

CREATING SPACE

During my five-month of sabbatical time at Pendle Hill in 1984 I attended Parker Palmer's *Tales of the Journey* course once a week. The previous summer I'd met Parker through his new book, *To Know as We Are Known: A Spirituality of Education.*[16] The pedagogy, sharing emanating from silence, which he described in his book, bore a resemblance to what I later found in Quaker worship sharing and still later in Buddhist *dharma* (referring to the teachings of the Buddha) sharing. Each provided a spiritual container in which it was possible to share suffering as well as joy. I'd already undergone life-changing encounters in alternative education with Ron McKeen, David Mallery, and St. Mary's. I felt at home and well nourished by Parker's style. At the end of each class he'd give us an aphorism related to journeys which we were invited to write about in the coming week. The reflections we did primed us to share from our depths when we gathered again as a class. The space Parker opened for us and helped us to hold together, helped each of us touch our truth in that moment. We were able to speak our own personal truth and listen deeply to the truth of others, to what was alive in that moment, listening obediently, devotedly, and with fidelity.

The space that Parker created was co-created by us students. This was true for the whole Pendle Hill community—in our daily Quaker worship after breakfast, our daily service helping to cook, put out meals, and clean up, and our weekly chores. For me cleaning ovens every Wednesday morning for three months with Bill Tabor was my first contemplative activity. Everything about Pendle Hill's space supported deep learning.

The same had been true at St. Mary's, but there we'd had challenges. One was staffing. Our unique practices could be difficult to convey to potential staff members. Attracted to our vision, some staff members were then confronted by their ingrained ways of thinking and acting. During the summer of 1980, St. Mary's Center faced what initially felt like a crisis. We'd hired Andy, an active member of the anti-nuclear movement, as a counselor. I invited my friend Bob Civiak, a nuclear energy expert with the Congressional Research Service, to visit both St. Mary's sessions and debate Andy on nuclear power. Our first-session debate was a disaster. While Bob presented arguments based on scientific findings, Andy's rebuttals were muddy and emotional. After Bob left, students reported that Andy told them Bob had lied about some facts. During the debate he'd said no such thing. When Andy's public accusations came to light, Jay called an emergency faculty meeting. I'd never participated in wiser or more vivid sharing. As teachers in this special program, we'd always understood ourselves to be in fundamental agreement. Now we tried honestly to express our deeply held, personal views. After several hours of deep listening and sharing we came up with a declaration of intent:

St. Mary's Center ~ 1980

The following ideas concerning the philosophy and goals of the St. Mary's Center were developed during a staff brainstorming session.

We believe that the St. Mary's Center should ...

- encourage and develop *critical* and *creative* thinking processes which can be *transferred* to new situations
- function as a *learning community* which encourages *growth* for both students *and* staff members (development of individual potential)
- encourage *open-mindedness* and *broadened* perspectives
- emphasize group *cooperation* over individual competition ("the whole can be greater than the sum of its parts"); promote an understanding of *group processes*
- encourage *holistic* thinking; emphasize *interrelationships* (and connections!) among various disciplines

- make learning *and* teaching challenging, stimulating, and enjoyable
- strive for Excellence in all areas – make *Quality* the norm
- encourage *positive* thinking
- develop an atmosphere of *trust* which encourages *risk taking*
- stimulate a sense of *social responsibility*, encouraging the application of skills and ideas developed at the Center (networking)
- promote a community which embodies the aforementioned goals[17]

This philosophy and these goals were the lived reality of our center, the space for living and learning we'd created. Articulating them so clearly deepened our appreciation of what we were engaged in. The newly written goals told incoming staff what to expect and how to support our center's mission. They applied equally to teaching and counseling. I felt tremendously grateful to have worked together to articulate a vision we all agreed with. One of our Environmental Science teachers replaced Andy for the second debate.

Many years later, creating space for inward exploration and deep sharing was one of my primary goals for the eight-day educator retreats I led at Centro Avalokita in Italy. There the practice of Noble Silence was central. These were times of no talking meant to enable us to connect with ourselves and others from a place of stillness. After an initial week-long immersion in the Avalokita experience, I returned a second summer with many ideas. One was that we'd wait until the second day to introduce ourselves and share our gifts. The first evening we'd begin by slowly eating one raisin in mindfulness after which I'd begin to introduce basic mindfulness practice. We'd close the evening with partners taking turns holding each other's hand in silence, the practice I'd learned in Plum Village twenty-three years earlier.

This worked well. However, at the opening staff meeting, I made what turned out to be a fateful decision. Stefano, the senior resident teacher, inquired about Noble Silence, scheduled to start at the end of the evening program every day. When should it end? Feeling the collective energy of the staff members around me, I suggested Noble Silence end after lunch the following day.

From the beginning of the retreat, people balked at the amount of silence. I watched conversations take place during outdoor walking meditation. I heard a group returning to Avalokita at 10:00 p.m., one night audibly finishing their conversation outside the building. There were complaints in *dharma* sharing groups about too much Noble Silence. I was upset. Friends on staff told me to relax. Italians love to talk, teachers most of all. I didn't know how to repair the breakdown of silence, but I didn't want to accept things as they were.

I needed to understand the situation more deeply. Drawing on an experience with my algebra class many years before, the following day I gave each participant a slip of paper.

> On one side of your paper please write "yes" or "no" as your answer to the question, "Do you engage in conversations during Noble Silence?" If your answer is "yes," please write the reasons why you do so on the other side of your paper.

When I read what they'd written, the results were clear. A large majority of the participants indicated they had conversations. The overwhelming reason was that the other participants were special, very different from teachers at home. There just wasn't enough time to talk to these wonderful new teacher friends. There was also a group of participants who always observed Noble Silence. Would it be possible to come up with a solution which would satisfy everyone?

Stefano scheduled two hours for my talk the next day. I began by recounting the results of the previous day's survey and telling the group that I didn't know how to proceed. I had no choice but to let go. I was aware of three ways of doing this. The first was acceptance. The second was to ask myself, "Am I sure?" The third was to stop making an effort and to turn the job over to the Buddha. I'd ruled out the first. The second seemed a dead end. I would try the third. As Thây often told his students, the community would be the next Buddha. I told participants I was turning the problem over to them. Each person would have a chance to share thoughts and feelings, and the group would try to find a resolution that met the needs of all.

Out of the quiet of the meditation hall, everyone shared. For one retreatant, silence had ceased to be a rule and had become a refuge. Another understood the value silence had for others and suggested designating a meeting and talking area outside the building. This was a popular proposal, but in the end, it was clear that doing so would divide the group in two, much as smoking and nonsmoking teachers' lounges had once divided the faculty in Italian schools. A proposal to end Noble Silence after breakfast the next and final day of the retreat was endorsed by everyone.

I returned to Avalokita to teach a third time in July 2016. This time Stefano sent me a message beforehand: What did I want to do about Noble Silence? After much thought I suggested we leave the decision to the retreatants. The first evening I informed the new group that "rest" would be the following day's focus. I continued, "Our minds need rest as well as our bodies. When we talk, we don't give our minds much chance to rest. Tomorrow we'll observe Noble Silence through the end of lunch, then enjoy a period of total relaxation in which we'll progressively invite parts of our bodies, beginning with our toes and moving up to the top of our heads, to relax. Following that, we'll decide how much silence we'll observe for the rest of the retreat."

The next afternoon the group assembled to search for unity on the question of whether to extend silence through lunch or end it earlier. Our group of sixteen included five people entirely new to mindfulness practice. One woman told us that since she didn't know anyone else there, she needed to talk to make connections. Another said that staying silent even through breakfast was a stretch. Another needed to call her children every morning. However, one new practitioner found this a rare opportunity to explore quiet. She didn't want to miss it. Long-time retreatants chimed in. In the end, the group agreed to observe Noble Silence through lunch each day. Necessary conversations could take place outside the building where we lived and met. The opening day-of-silence had established a feeling. Although not everyone observed the decision thoroughly, the power of the group process created a strong retreat with a profound sense of community.

REFLECTIONS AND CONTEMPLATIONS

Contemplate a learning setting that was important to you as a student. As a teacher.

What made them important?

Recall a significant experience of silence and return to it.

Why was it significant?

NOTES

1 Todd, M. L. (Ed.) (1894). *Letters of Emily Dickinson.* Boston: Roberts Brothers, 316.

2 Oliver, M. (1990). "The Summer Day" in *House of Light.* Boston: Beacon Press, 60.

3 Parnes, S. J. (1981). *The magic of your mind.* Buffalo: Creative Education Foundation.

4 Joanna Ziegler, Personal Communication, 2009.

5 Earl Harrison, "In Memory of Earl Harrison," Sidwell Friends, accessed October 30, 2020, https://www.sidwell.edu/retired-former-employees/tributes/~board/news-tributes/post/in-memory-of-earl-harrison

6 Adapted from Brady, R. and McHenry, I. (Eds.) (2009). "The magic eye: Tuning in during meeting for worship" in *Tuning in: Mindfulness in teaching and learning.* Philadelphia: Friends Council on Education, 81–82.

7 Although this quote is frequently attributed to psychiatrist Viktor Frankl, its origin has not been determined. See https://quoteinvestigator.com/2018/02/18/response/, accessed October 10, 2020,for more information.

8 This exercise is described in detail in Peggy Smith,"Where Am I," Open Communication, accessed October 10, 2020, http://www.opencommunication.org/articles/WhichChair-ChoiceFromSelfAwareness.pdf.

9 For more information on universal human needs and Nonviolent Communication, see Rosenberg, M. (2015), *Nonviolent communication: A language of life,* Third Edition. Encinitas, CA: Puddle Dancer Press.

10 Kirshenbaum, M. and Foster, C. (1991). *Parent/teen breakthrough: The relationship approach.* New York: Plume.

11 Grubb, S. (1794). *Some Account of the Life and Religious Labours of Sarah Grubb,* Second Edition. London: James Phillips, 198.

12 For more information on the Myers-Briggs Type Indicator see: Wikipedia, "Myers-Briggs Type Indicator," accessed October 10, 2020, https://en.wikipedia.org/wiki/Myers%E2%80%93Briggs_Type_Indicator

13 Remen, R. N. (2000). *My Grandfather's Blessings: Stories of Strength, Refuge, and Belonging.* New York: Riverhead Books, 66–67.

14 Hanh, T.N. (1987). "Please Call Me by My True Names" in *Being Peace.* Berkeley: Parallax Press, 63–64.

15 Solzhenitsyn, A. (2007). *The Gulag Archipelago Volume 1: An Experiment in Literary Investigation.* New York: Harper Perennial Modern Classics, 75.

16 Palmer, P. (1983). *To Know as We are Known: A Spirituality of Education.* San Francisco: Harper & Row.

17 St. Mary's Instructional Staff, Personal Communication, 1980.

PART IV

WALKING MY PATH

Traveller, there is no path, the path is made by walking.

—Antonio Machado[1]

When I embarked on what would become my path as a teacher, as Machado suggests, there was none. I had no idea that I was making a path, much less, where it might lead. I had no expectations. I lived my teacher's life class by class, day by day. At the end of my first year of teaching, a group of Advanced Placement calculus students told me they'd worked ahead when they realized the class wouldn't be completing the full curriculum covered on the Advanced Placement exam. I had intentionally slowed the pace to make sure every student understood the material. Pulling myself up by my bootstraps the following year, I focused on pedagogy that demystified abstract concepts. However, I was uncomfortable standing in front of groups of students, some not needing to listen and others listening but not comprehending. The process of redefining myself as a facilitator of learning opened. This led me to guides and writers with whom I found resonance. I cobbled together strategies and approaches from small-group learning, problem solving, and remarkable textbooks, unaware that there might be a foundation that could support them all. When I was ready, I encountered Thich Nhat Hanh's teachings on mindfulness and found a home with my name on it. I was able to make sense of the path I'd been walking, and I walked on with awareness. Life had become my teacher.

While writing this book, I learned my dear friend Susan was in a coma with encephalitis of the brain. Several weeks later I was able to visit her. Susan had emerged from her coma, able only to move her feet and arms and turn her head. Her eyes were bright and connecting and she could quietly speak a few words. She was fighting gallantly to come back from the abyss. Three visits left me overwhelmed, a great heaviness in my heart. On the flight home I attempted to commit my grief to paper:

My Teacher

Life enters the hall,
and I rise.
She walks slowly
to the altar,
turns, and bows.
I bow to life.
The lesson is complete.

This poem was the result of more than my visit. Many years of life had prepared me for it. I'd been blessed with many teachers, Susan among them. Each helped me understand more of the life I was experiencing and prepared me for experiences to come. But, ultimately, my experiences had been my teacher and, when I had digested them, the meaning I made of them. These insights about meaning had always been most readily available to me in Plum Village.

Following my initial retreat with Thây at Plum Village in 1992, I knew I needed to return for a longer stay. Arranging for a leave from school, I registered to attend six weeks of the 1993–94 winter retreat—time to learn and reflect in the beautiful quiet countryside of southwest France. I began preparations for Plum Village that spring by joining a retreat on transformation at the Kripalu Center for Yoga and Health in Lenox, Massachusetts. There I had an opportunity to attend *satsang*—a meeting of disciples with their guru, Gurudev, Kripalu's spiritual leader at that time. Devotees dressed in white sat in the front, close to their teacher. I settled in just behind. Gurudev began playing hypnotic music on the harmonium, creating a sort of trance in the hall. When he asked for questions, I had one. So did a number of devotees in front of me. I raised my hand and looked Gurudev square in the face after he answered each query. Finally, he nodded to me.

I had my mother on my mind. The previous year, when I'd learned that Thây would be giving a public lecture in Chicago during his forthcoming North American tour, I encouraged my mother to attend. My mom's mind—always curious and filled with ideas—was anything but quiet. After she attended his teaching, I was interested to hear her response.

"Did you like Thich Nhat Hanh?" I asked.

"Yes, he was very nice."

"Was there anything in particular about his talk you remember?"

"Yes. He gave us a meditation to do that included the words, 'Breathing in I experience myself as still water; breathing out I reflect things just as they are.' My eyes were closed and suddenly I saw myself at midnight sitting silently with a fellow camper in a canoe in the middle of Blue Lake many years ago. The moon was reflecting on the calm water. It was so peaceful."

Mom's sweet memory was much like my own of the magical bonfire at my summer camp. If only, as she grew older, she'd pursued more such experiences, I thought.

Now at Kripalu reflecting on my inability to communicate my insights to my mom, I spoke to Gurudev.

"I've received great benefit from my spiritual practice. How can I share it with my mother?"

"You know the answer to that question", Gurudev replied.

I sat in the ensuing silence feeling confused and upset. Had he nothing more to say to me?

Finally, he spoke again. "Go and wash her car."

I was sad with the thought that I might have nothing to offer my mother from my precious spiritual path. I hoped my upcoming visit to Plum Village would yield a more encouraging answer.

When I arrived in Plum Village just after Christmas, the community was working on an assignment Thây had given everyone to complete by New Year's—creating lists of our beneficial and detrimental qualities. Thây requested we make the beneficial list longer. After completing the lists, we were to study each quality to see if we could discern its origin. I saw that a majority of the characteristics on both of my lists were present in my dad. I wasn't surprised. He was my outspoken male model. Many qualities came from Mom, too. Shortly before Dad died that fall, I'd thanked him for the many ways he'd contributed to our family. Mom was sitting in the room, but it hadn't occurred to me at the time to thank her as well. Now from Plum Village, I wrote from my heart, thanking her for all the positive traits she'd bequeathed me. When I called a couple of weeks later, she told me that when she'd read the letter, she'd cried. She asked me to thank my teacher. She only wished she'd written a letter like that to her own mother. I told her she still could. Just a few months after receiving Gurudev's instruction to wash my mom's car, life had given me a deeply meaningful way to share my practice with her.

Reflecting on life and learning from it had been central to me, and I was gratified to receive evidence that my students were similarly engaged. This was beautifully conveyed by one student when he wrote:

I have learned great things from myself in the way that I respond to quotes in my journal and in how I respond to myself in free writing. In writing continuously, I often write things that I did not understand consciously before they hit the paper.

Conscious understanding for me sometimes seemed to require years of unconscious incubation. When the conditions were right, understanding might arrive when I was writing a journal entry or a poem or simply lying in bed. The lessons life was giving me were completed in that moment. I revisited them again and again. Their meaning and their significance continued to grow in my unconscious and as they got evoked by new experience.

REFLECTIONS AND CONTEMPLATIONS

Give yourself a week to create lists of your beneficial and detrimental qualities. Make the beneficial one longer. When you've finished, look deeply at each quality to get in touch with its origins.

Contemplate a life lesson you've received.

What conditions contributed to your receiving it?

What is an important lesson you've passed on or would like to pass on?

THE CONDITIONS ARE PERFECT

The stimulus for one of many important lessons I've received arrived the week after Christmas in 1998 during my first visit to Green Mountain Monastery, Thây's center then in Vermont. When I got there, I was quite tired and unhappy. The fall had been a challenging time at home and at school. After three days of sitting meditation, eating meditation, and mindful walking in the quiet, snow-covered hills of Vermont, I relaxed and started smiling again. My primary concern was how to take this peace home with me. Hoping for advice and reassurance, I asked Sister Annabel, the Monastery's Abbess, for a consultation. I began by describing my return home from previous retreats.

> "When I get home, I'm walking on air, Sister Annabel, but I'm like a tire with a slow leak. Friends meeting me a week or so after my return don't know I've been anywhere. How can I keep my practice alive?"

Sister Annabel laughed, then, looking me in the eyes, she said,

> "Richard, you know this practice is the practice of the present moment. The Maryland present moment is different from the Vermont present moment. You are present in both places, but all the other causes and conditions are different. Don't expect to bring Vermont back to Maryland."

Sister Annabel paused, giving me time to feel my sadness and resignation, then continued:

"Here's the good news: The causes and conditions in Maryland
are perfect for the practice that needs to be done there."

This came as a ray of hope but left me with a question:
What exactly was the practice that needed to be done in Maryland?
Returning home, I was still pretty much in the dark. Being able
to find appropriate responses to difficulties at home or in school
required that I understand their nature and that I had sufficient
experience of practice to draw on. The benefits of aging include
the accumulation of experience and growth of understanding that
has come with it. Sometimes this is sufficient to meet a new challenge, as the following story reveals:

At the 1982 Creative Problem Solving Institute (CPSI) in
Buffalo, a complex interpersonal problem occurred. Mornings
at CPSI began with home group meetings. Each group had a
theme, enabling those with common interests to come together.
That year my home group focused on creative process. At its
organizational meeting, the leader explained that every morning
several of us would present an aspect of the creative process—for
example, *humor*. Later that day group members would wear met-
aphorical humor glasses to watch for the presence of wit. When
we gathered the next morning, we'd share the results, then don a
new pair of glasses for the next aspect—for example, *curiosity*. The
leader read the list of suggested creativity aspects. Almost as an
afterthought, he mentioned that Frank had proposed *spirituality*.
He wondered if there were others who would like to join Frank's
group and seemed surprised when several hands went up.

Three of us joined Frank to make plans for the following
morning. We were aware of several possible challenges. One was
that we wanted everyone to focus on the topic. We decided
on an interactive presentation. But how could we engage the
cynics? I recalled an experience when CPSI was drawing to a
close the previous year. I'd overheard a business consultant say
to a group of friends,

After I describe the transformation that Creative Problem
Solving leads to, people again and again say it reminds them
of the same thing. Would you like to guess what that is?

Their wrong answers ranged from *the Quakers* to *Martin Luther King Jr.*

It reminds them of *the Force* from *Star Wars.*

My intuition told me that in this fertile setting *the Force* would be with everyone.

Our home group would meet first thing the next morning. We knew folks would drift in and want to sit with friends and chat. To avoid this, we drew on a practice from one of David Mallery's workshops. As people entered, we directed them to form groups of four. Once their group was complete, we asked them as a group to take turns sharing their understanding or experience of *the Force.* Eventually, we asked the entire home group to stand in a circle and share out of the silence, speaking to the whole group as in Quaker worship sharing. We never mentioned spirituality. Sharings went deep—many spiritual in nature. As portrayed in *Star Wars,* the Force for me was a feeling of connection, of no longer existing as a separate entity, of being interwoven with the whole universe. I'd felt the presence of the Force sitting overnight with my brother Bob in an island hospital nine years before. I'd felt it during an evening with Ram Dass, in the midst of Grateful Dead concerts, and in Meetings for Worship. I knew it was accessible to everyone. It belonged to everyone.

My life had given me resources to draw on in responding to our *spirituality* challenge. This was not unusual. Shortly after I returned to teaching at Sidwell Friends following my sabbatical year at Buffalo State and Pendle Hill, I was approached by Marsha, the coordinator for Quaker life. Our Principal had appraised Marsha of a serious conflict between two students and invited her to resolve it. Marsha asked for my help. Samuel, a 10th grader from an Armenian family, was very involved politically. Recently, he'd put up a poster on a school bulletin board commemorating International Holocaust Remembrance Day. It described the 1915 Armenian genocide at the hands of the Ottoman government. The poster disturbed Leda, also a 10th grader. Her Turkish family asked the Principal to remove it. Though that initial poster went down, a second poster went up. After that poster was taken down, Samuel gave a message in Sidwell's Meeting for Worship condoning terrorism as a tactic for bringing injustice to world attention. He also wrote an article for the school paper about the Armenian genocide. What to do?

At Pendle Hill I'd learned about the Quaker practice of "clearness committees."[2] When one or two "focus" people reach an impasse with a decision or conflict, a small group or clearness committee is called together to help discern the way to proceed. Marsha agreed that this approach was worth trying, so we met individually with Leda and Samuel. We explained to them the goals of a clearness committee, how Marsha and I would be members them and would invite them to add two other students approved by both of them. Samuel was happy to have a forum to justify his actions. Leda did not want to be involved in a confrontation. She was hesitant to participate at all until we assured her the committee would confine itself to asking questions and she and Samuel would direct their answers to the committee, not to each other. We all hoped that greater understanding of the whole truth in this situation would lead to healing. Leda and Samuel each made a list of six or seven classmates who might serve on their committee. Then each chose one participant from the other's list.

Marsha reserved a private room in the school library for a Saturday morning. Anticipating a long meeting, we ordered pizza and sodas delivered around lunchtime. We gathered. For over an hour the meeting proceeded as it has been laid out. However, Samuel and Leda responded as if they weren't even in the same room, Samuel issuing political rhetoric and Leda proclaiming the irrelevance of contested events of 1915 to the conduct of the present Sidwell Friends community. When movement finally occurred, it followed a breach in the guidelines. Jill, a student member of the committee, began speaking to Leda and Samuel, pointing out to them that besides being members of the same class, both were sensitive, caring people with strong interests in the arts. "Were it not for an historical ethnic conflict," Jill said, "you might be the best of friends!" Following this, Leda turned to Samuel and told him directly that she couldn't understand how someone his age could already be "filled with so much hate." Samuel didn't seem at all prepared for this reflection of himself in Leda's eyes. When he responded, his edge had melted. "I'm not filled with hate," he said. "I was simply trying to raise student consciousness about the past so they would work for peace and justice in the future." Leda was able to agree with Samuel's goals but pled for other ways to accomplish them. The conflict evaporated and Samuel, Leda, and the committee came together with a common purpose. We agreed to close the meeting and meet again to generate some ideas and determine a plan of action. The action turned out to be inviting two speakers familiar with Turkish and Armenian history to visit Sidwell and speak to interested Upper School students and faculty about lessons to be learned from that past.

Since then I've been a member of more clearness committees and a focus person for a few. It's essential that a person familiar with this practice serve as the convener of a clearness committee. This enables newcomers to be guided by an experienced hand, often someone with a Quaker background.

Conditions present in most challenging situations don't suggest the use of clearness committees. To know "the practice that needs to be done there," familiarity with a variety of practices is important. I'm always on the lookout for new ones. When friends in Boston invited me to offer a day of mindfulness following a tragedy which had affected them all, I chose the theme *Joy*. Before the day arrived, a friend, learning of the theme, wrote to ask if I was familiar with *The Book of Joy*, by HH the Dalai Lama and Archbishop Desmond Tutu. Two days later, I was infused with their smiling faces and their wise teachings, in particular their guided meditation "The Eight Pillars." This meditation became my practice in times of challenge and a staple of my teaching. It begins with selecting a difficulty or source of suffering. Meditators proceed to contemplate their challenge through eight lenses: *Perspective, Humility, Humor, Acceptance, Forgiveness, Gratitude, Compassion*, and *Generosity*. The beginning of the contemplations on Perspective and Forgiveness follow:

> **Perspective.** *See yourself and your problem from a wider perspective. Try to step back from yourself and your problem. See yourself and your struggle as if you were in a movie.*
>
> **Forgiveness.** *Place your hand on your heart and forgive yourself for any part you have played in creating this problem or this situation.*[3]

These quiet contemplations require space and time. In my experience, they usually bear fruit—ease, insight, even joy.

REFLECTIONS AND CONTEMPLATIONS

How have conditions at home and school determined practices you've employed there?

Recall a time when you benefitted from the support of others in discerning a solution to a problem—return to and dwell with that experience.

How and where do you find practices that support you?

WELL-BEING AND HAPPINESS

Back in the days when saber-toothed tigers roamed the Earth, humans always needed to be on the alert for danger. Anxiety and vigilance were the default channels of their brains. Likely there was little time for happiness. We've inherited our brains from these ancestors, including their "negativity bias." In today's world, this contributes to a great deal of unnecessary anxiety. However, our brains are plastic, i.e. able to change. Recalling past times of happiness and listening to stories of happiness from others increases the signal strength of our happiness channel. Expanding our awareness of sources of happiness in the present moment is even more beneficial. I've often invited educators to make lists of these sources and to add to them over time. Their lists have included: loved ones, nature, pets, music, art, and blue skies. The sources tend to be external. Thich Nhat Hanh regularly asked retreatants to recall having a toothache. Then he'd inquire, "Weren't you happy when your toothache went away?" Of course, we were! He'd then conclude with, "How many of you are happy that you don't have toothaches now?" He knew what a tremendous asset emotional resilience was for all of us. Building our mindfulness on a foundation of happiness gives us the strength we need to care for the suffering we also carry,

Teaching in Boston I offered *The Eight Pillars* meditation with its focus on addressing ill-being. I accompanied it with an opportunity for participants to immerse themselves in happiness. *Blue Skies Practice*, which I learned from my friend John Bell, began with our group singing Irving Berlin's popular song *Blue Skies*.[4] The group then created a list of words that described "blue sky" times. Next, we all closed our eyes and for several minutes contemplated "blue sky" times in our lives, finally selecting one of them. Opening our eyes, we found a partner and took turns, sharing our happiness for three minutes.

With students, I've looked for more hands-on experiences of happiness. One of my best discoveries was the game Jenga.[5] This game involves successively removing one of fifty-four stacked, wooden blocks from a lower level of three blocks and placing it on the top level, trying to build the tower as high as possible before it crashes down. As the tower rises, its foundation becomes more delicate. Greater concentration and care are needed to remove blocks. I introduced Jenga to my homeroom students— some already knew it—as a way to work together on a challenge. The activity promoted mindfulness and solidarity as we each took our turn and gave advice to others. Tension rose along with the tower. There was a bit of embarrassment for the one who wasn't able to remove the last block safely, making the game that much more fun—a happy way to begin an intense day of learning.

Happiness is no stranger to Plum Village retreats. Informal tea ceremonies featuring song, musical performance, dance, poetry, and skits often lighten the intensity of the dharma talks and meditation. Plum Village is also the setting where I was confronted by personal challenges of transformation of my own and others suffering into happiness. Here is one of my successes:

During the 2014 June retreat in Plum Village I was especially interested in attending a gathering of educators from Asia as I'd been invited to give a keynote talk on education at a conference in Hong Kong the following year. Twenty-five of us arrived at the place, which David, the organizer, had reserved. In the center of "our" space, we found three prone bodies. We sat and waited for them to rise and depart. Indistinguishable words issued from their CD player. As I chatted quietly with one of my neighbors, I heard David ask someone to gently rouse the guests. We were ready to begin our sharing. I didn't notice what happened next, but following their departure, David asked us to take a few moments to send them positive energy.

Five hours later, I'd just washed my lunch dishes when two of the three retreatants who'd been invited to leave approached me. At this moment Henri was obviously incensed. "You're the one responsible for the group and you're a Dharma Teacher. You understand what 'interbeing' means, yet you interrupt our meditation when we're almost finished!" Henri went on in this way for some time. I just listened, breathed, and embraced him with compassion in my heart. When he paused, I apologized on behalf of our group. "I'm so sorry. I understand why you're upset. I'll convey your unhappiness to the organizer of the meeting when I see him." Henri calmed down, I bowed to him and Celeste, and we parted ways.

Near the end of outdoor walking meditation the following day, we heard the sound of a bell inviting us to stop, breathe, and enjoy our surroundings. I turned around and saw Henri and Celeste a few feet away. Without hesitating, I approached them, looked Henri in the eye and said, "You are more beautiful today than you were yesterday." He smiled. We bowed to each other. On the final morning of the retreat, as I was preparing a sandwich to take along for lunch, I spied Henri and Celeste at the other end of the dining hall. They approached me. Without words, we bowed to one another and hugged mindfully. The lesson was complete.

Plum Village always nurtured my happiness and well-being, making deeply rewarding experiences possible. Life has been rewarding all along my path, my dis-ease as well as my happiness. I do my best to maintain balance through the highs and lows with daily practice—on awakening, bringing to mind three things from the day before for which I'm grateful, then doing the Chinese healing practice *qigong* and once again before going to bed. Supporting each other, my partner Elisabeth and I take turns reading inspiring poems and stories before going to bed, deepening our connection to each other and to life. As I was writing this book, a preschool educator friend suggested I read works by Vivian Gussin Paley. Our local library had a copy of *The Girl with the Brown Crayon*.[6] Soon Elisabeth and I were reading it nightly. We're now completing our sixth of Vivian's books, crying one minute, laughing the next as we inhale her accounts of life with preschool and kindergarten children.

REFLECTIONS AND CONTEMPLATIONS

Get in touch with your happiness at this moment. Savor it.

Make a list of causes that come to mind. Add additional ones as they occur to you.

Reflect on how you've promoted happiness at work—your own and others.

Recall a time when you found a bit of happiness or joy in a difficult situation—your own or others.

What supported this? What were some outcomes?

CAUSES AND CONDITIONS

Happiness, like everything else, is impermanent. It arises when causes and conditions are sufficient and departs when they cease to be. These changes may occur over a period of time or happen in an instant. For me the latter was the case in 1993 during a yearlong meditation/therapy course led by meditation teacher Tara Brach. That year began and ended with weekend retreats. In between, we had once a month, daylong meetings. When I signed up, I had no idea that the therapy component would be psychodrama. Once during that year I was the focus person or protagonist. This entailed having group members enact an incident from my life, someone else playing my part. I chose the theme of the drama—my family's unexpressed grief. As I watched the actors play out this deep thread in my family of origin, I felt overwhelmed—even after the drama ended. My joy disappeared, and life became two-dimensional. On the edge of depression, I looked for professional help. I asked friends to recommend a helper who drew on Eastern wisdom. Two suggested Rudy Bauer, a therapist and yogi. *Rudy* was my dad's name. I had no doubt about the rightness of this recommendation.

At our first session, hearing about my suffering, Rudy asked me to identify someone I loved unconditionally. "My daughter, Shoshanna," I readily replied. Rudy asked me to bring Shoshanna into my heart and feel the support of her presence. He then invited me to focus my awareness on the energy in my body, guiding me here and there, asking for feedback. He instructed, "Tolerate this, tolerate that, just tolerate it, don't think, don't judge." Several times he said, "It's no big deal." I began to get back in touch with my loving self. Rudy explained afterwards that working with "histor-ical material" might be the right thing to do in the future. But, he added, "Richard, your center is currently so weak, you could easily become overwhelmed feeling your emotions." As Rudy saw it, his job was to help me solidify my own emotional grounding.

For five months I visited Rudy weekly. Our work was often meditative in nature, Rudy always keeping energetic contact with me. When my eyes were closed I could still feel his presence. Once he climbed up on the sofa behind me, pressed his knees into my back, and pulled my shoulders backward. For ten minutes, he held me in this position helping me tune into my strength. Another time he connected me with my passion by asking me to close my eyes and listen to Indian devotional chants. "As you listen," Rudy instructed, "don't visualize anyone outside yourself as the source of your passion. Your passion is in you. It's not dependent on anyone else." Another meditation put me in touch with my inner spaciousness. This was my introduction to tuning into pos-itive channels through meditation, a practice I later shared with ninth graders.

My depression eventually lifted, and Rudy invited me to attend one of his groups. When I arrived at one session feeling joyless, Rudy asked three group members to grab my arms and waist and pull me in different directions. Trying to resist, I erupted in screams that soon turned into belly laughter. At last, here was my body's hidden joy! None of the work with Rudy ever touched upon the "historical material" that took me to see him in the first place. Later I'd be ready to encounter the past.

Transforming my relationship to my past happened in another way, very different from my time with Rudy. It began in Plum Village, the place where over years I learned many of the most important lessons of my life. I first heard of Plum Village in 1989 during my first retreat with Thây at Omega Institute in upstate New York. A woman in our dharma sharing group told us this was her first experience with meditation. Tears were coming to her eyes every time she meditated. She went on to say that her life was happy and she'd had no traumas in her past. She won-dered whether her situation was normal. If this was what medita-tion was like, she wasn't sure that she wanted to continue. People who responded told her that her experience was not so unusual.

One said, with a bit of humor, that in Plum Village, Thich Nhat Hanh's community in France, there was a rule against crying for more than five minutes. It was not uncommon, he added, to find Westerners sobbing in the bushes.

In the years that followed, I experienced intense emotion many times—including tears—during my visits to Plum Village. Sometimes I was alone, sometimes with others. One of these moments will always be with me. It was a dharma sharing group with two other men. During the previous dharma sharing, James had shared that ever since coming to Plum Village he'd felt he'd been carrying the weight of the world on his shoulders. He couldn't account for this feeling. During the question and answer session the next day, James told Thây that his brother had died of suicide and asked him for advice. Thây responded that each of us has the seed of suicide and the seed of joy inside us. Which of these seeds sprouts depends on which is watered. Thây went on to say that from what James had shared, it was clear that the seed of suicide had been watered in him. James was at risk. He needed to examine carefully his life choices (his home, his job, his friends) and change any elements that were not watering his seeds of joy.

That evening our dharma sharing group met again. There were just three of us. Our sharing soon turned to the question James asked that afternoon. James added that earlier in his life he'd had problems with alcohol. His sister-in-law was the only person who'd supported him then. Two years after James' brother took his life, this sister-in-law, during a period of profound depression, had also taken her life, leaving two small children. We were listening deeply, holding him in our hearts.

Following James' story, William told us about his brother, a doctor. Two years earlier, his brother had developed an aggressive brain tumor. William booked a flight to visit him but was told by his brother, whose mood the tumor had considerably darkened, not to come. With ticket in hand, William decided to ignore his brother's wishes and go. At the end of his long flight, he was met by his grief-stricken nephew. William's brother, pessimistic about the future of the world, had taken the life of his wife and then killed himself.

Our group fell into an extended period of silence. Tears were flowing. We knew that this suffering was not just personal, not even the suffering of our generation. It came from our ancestors as well, suffering that had been denied, hidden behind stern and proper behavior, held at bay by living lives protected from feelings. Now the suffering had burst into the open. For the three of us it was inescapable. Together we held all this suffering knowing it was on behalf of our ancestors and future generations. At Plum Village, we'd learned to touch both our ancestors and our descendants through the practice of meditation. Now we were able to experience our ancestors' suffering as our own as well.

After some time had passed, I began to share the story of my younger brother, Bob, my only sibling. As a teenager, he had a series of physical and psychological problems. Eventually Bob's condition led him to drop out of school, leave our home in Illinois, and move to California where he hoped to regain his health. He ate fresh fruit and vegetables, took supplements, and exercised, but was unsuccessful. After returning home, Bob became attracted to fasting as a way to cleanse his body of toxins. He began a supervised water fast at a health center in Texas. After forty-five days, the medical staff advised Bob to stop. Not willing to follow their advice, he continued for fifteen more days. Two days after completing the fast, Bob went into a coma. He came out of the coma with a stiff hip and brain damage that severely impaired his short-term memory and left him subject to seizures. Since then Bob had lived with our parents or in one of several communities for people with mental disabilities. He referred to this experience as his first life, his death, and his second life.

My sharing with James and William was the first time I'd ever told my brother's story and been able to feel my grief fully. Through our tears, we contacted a truth beyond suffering. We'd learned from Thây to embrace and cradle suffering as we would a crying infant. I'd done this in the past in other conducive environments, supported by spiritual friends, and had experienced emotional healing from it. Whatever liberation we might achieve now through our practice, we would be sharing with the next generation: James with his young niece and nephew as well as his own son; William with his son and his grown nephews, and I with my daughter. We were in Plum Village, home to many joyful monks and nuns, many of whom were Vietnamese refugees who'd experienced tremendous suffering. Thây had shown them how to water the seeds of joy as well as how to hold their suffering. In the depth of our connection with them and with each other, we found ourselves touching our own seeds of joy.

Many years have passed since that experience. My process of opening to suffering continues. It has become easier to touch my suffering and that of others. Sometimes, when I'm able to hold emotional upheavals in my current relationships with awareness, doors to old pain open. Tension in my body has also connected me to old fears and anger. I've learned to be with both old and new suffering in an accepting way, to hold it with the help of my ancestors and descendants. It's no longer just mine. I feel lighter, happier, and more alive.[7]

REFLECTIONS AND CONTEMPLATIONS

How have you practiced with your own historical material?

When have you chosen not to practice with historical material?

Contemplate a time when you practiced with your current suffering.

Recall a time when you experienced joy and pain as one.

RIPENING

Conflict is another area where transformation can take place when conditions change. Faculty conflicts have been of special interest to me. Award-giving was a deep concern I brought to my work as an educator from my own high school days. Just before graduation, New Trier High School's class of 1962 was invited into the school auditorium for an awards assembly. This came as a surprise to me and my classmates. When the Rensselaer Medal for best work in mathematics and science was announced, I thought of several friends who merited it. I was more embarrassed than pleased when I was invited on stage. I was uncomfortable being singled out.

At Sidwell Friends on the day before Upper School graduation, we devoted a full morning to awards. The athletic department handed out awards for overall achievement. Honors were bestowed upon the best of the best for overall academic achievement as well as excellence in every discipline. Students didn't know ahead of time who would receive awards, but parents of recipients were called in advance and invited to attend the ceremony.

I was sad that as the senior class emerged into the world, they were divided into those who received awards and those who did not. Equality was a Quaker testimony. It doesn't suggest that all people are the same; some do have special talents. However, our differences are far less significant than "that of God," which we all have in common. With this in mind, on two occasions over a period of five or six years I joined with like-minded Upper School faculty to take our concerns about awards before the whole faculty for consideration.

The process of choosing recipients was a mixed bag, easy when one student's participation and achievements stood out. More often, there were several outstanding students. Choosing just one could be trying, even acrimonious for faculty. Parents who believed their children deserved an award and didn't get one were bitterly disappointed. Students already knew which of their peers were accomplished. The college admissions process was over. Transcripts and teachers' letters of recommendation had already proven their worthiness. Why the extra accolades? Why did we highlight competition? The second time the Sidwell faculty considered this question, we had more support for doing away with awards, yet nothing close to unity. A number of influential faculty members still favored them.

The two previous times we'd raised the question of giving awards were at the beginning of a school year when the downside of the awards process had faded from consciousness. After waiting several years, I took a cue from Ronald Heifetz' book, *Leadership without Easy Answers*.[8] I asked our Principal, Bryan Garman, to include the topic of awards on the agenda for our year-end faculty meetings. Bryan inquired why I thought it made sense to bring it up a third time. "Heifetz posits that situations must be ripe for change before people are ready to support it," I told Bryan, "and, from what I've heard about this year's awards decision-making, the situation is ripe." Bryan concurred.

Our faculty discussion began with the usual view that it was our responsibility to celebrate excellence. Soon several senior faculty who previously had supported awards began to express reservations. The discussion took on a new tone. Teachers who seldom shared began to speak. People on both sides of the issue were listening deeply. Eventually Bryan stated his personal reservations. Those in favor of awards began to soften their opposition. In the end, only two people remained unconvinced. Both of them chose to stand aside, allowing the faculty as a group to move forward. I felt grateful for my trust in inner guidance and my contribution to our school, especially to our young people.

Grades, the most ubiquitous awards, were always problematic for me. In 1973 when I first arrived at Sidwell Friends, the Upper School sent home grade reports six times a year. The grades on each semester's first two progress reports were unofficial. Only the final semester grades appeared on transcripts. Writing these reports could require many hours. Rather than write comments, some teachers used check lists to rate students on competencies. A few years after my arrival, our faculty prevailed on the Principal to revise the system. I volunteered to join a small committee that would codify feedback from the faculty and draft a proposal. Our Principal required that comments from teachers be included with grades. So, the faculty agreed that reports would be sent home four times a year—progress reports without grades at the end of the first and third quarters—reports with grades and comments written at the end of each semester. This system stayed in place for the next ten years. Then, during year-end faculty meetings Principal Clint Wilkins proposed that our system be revised to include "advisory" grades on first and third quarter reports. We need these indicators, he told us, because some ninth graders and newly arrived students have been surprised, even upset by their first semester grades. "They need to know how they're doing sooner."

I asked how this could be. We consistently graded students on their tests, quizzes, and papers. How could they not know where they stood? Colleagues assured me otherwise—that students needed the grades, especially at the end of the first quarter. Thinking back to my eighth graders, I remembered how much students could improve during their first semester. First quarter grades could be problematic. Some students might be spurred to work harder, but others might see in grades a judgment not only of their work, but of themselves.

"Let's give our students a full semester to figure out how to do their best before we attach letters to them," I argued. No one agreed. In fact, one teacher angrily turned to me saying, "Do you mean to tell me that you would withhold information about my son from me?" His mind was closed. Alone in my objections, I refused to stand aside. I could not with integrity assign first quarter grades. After an hour, Clint shelved the discussion until the following day.

Clint wasn't a Quaker. Had he been familiar with Quaker process, he'd have known that "unity" doesn't necessarily mean "unanimity." When almost everyone is united on a decision, the clerk of the meeting may sense that a decision with which one or two disagree has nevertheless been reached. If the dissenters choose not to stand aside, the decision can still go forward with their views recorded. I had twenty-four hours to reflect on what had just transpired. Had this disagreement occurred in the context of a Friends Meeting for Business, I might have received calls or even visits from one or two Friends to help me discern a way forward. I had no such expectation. It was on me.

I based my semester grades on tests, quizzes, homework, and class participation. My students provided feedback on my comments. They needed to know how they were doing, and how they were doing was subject to change. It wasn't unusual for students' second semester grades to be higher or lower than their first. I recalled my own dramatic improvement in Mr. Boyle's senior English class. I saw grades as symbolizing a permanence that belied the dynamic nature of students' work. It would be more realistic to offer students a grade range, such as B-C, on quarter reports. This would serve as a heads-up to students and their parents. I could support the use of grade ranges. I found Clint before the start of our meeting the following day and made my proposal. He supported it. Later the rest of the faculty approved grade ranges as well. I came away with a deep respect for Quaker business practice and much gratitude for standing up for my own beliefs.

REFLECTIONS AND CONTEMPLATIONS

Recall a situation in your life that needed to ripen before change was possible.

What contributed to that ripening?

Contemplate a time when you stood up for an unpopular cause.

What was your experience?

Describe it to another person.

TIME TO SAY GOODBYE

If I've learned one thing as an educator, it's that change is possible, change at the institutional level, the class level, and the individual level. Actually, change is happening all the time. It may not be occurring at the conscious level. It may be small. It may go unnoticed. But it is happening.

Sometimes rituals that celebrate beginnings like the production of an opera or the sharing of gifts set the stage for change. Similarly, rituals that celebrate endings can confirm the changes that have occurred. The last day of my eight-day educator retreats in Italy has always been emotional. Each day we've sung a Plum Village practice song related to the theme of the day. The theme on our final day has been *No coming. No going.* Our practice song has this same title:

No Coming, No Going

No coming, no going
No after, no before
I hold you close to me
I release you to be so free
Because I am in you
And you are in me
Because I am in you
And you are in me[9]

Indeed, over the years, educator retreat participants in Italy have increasingly become like family. Last year the word many chose to describe their retreat experience was *inclusivity*.

Our closings have had a special ritual which begins with a recording of *Con te partirò* (*Time to say goodbye*), sung in Italian and English by Italian tenor Andrea Bocelli and English soprano Sarah Brightman.[10] After a few moments of silence, I invite the participants to close their eyes and let their minds review the last eight days beginning with seeing their arrival, the silent meals, early morning meditations, workshops, connections with others, and so on, letting the retreat unfold like a film with its times of practice, its chance meetings, its conversations. After they've revisited all that's happened, they return to one particular moment, a moment of special inspiration, a moment with particular energy, and hang out there. I learned this workshop-closing newsreel practice from David Mallery and have used it many times. Several minutes later, I sound a bell and ask participants to find a partner. Each person shares whatever wants to be shared for five minutes, a partner listening deeply. The hall is alive with animated speech and profound silence. The retreat's rich experience has been mined and honored.

At St. Mary's Center, each session concluded with an evening commencement where both a counselor and an instructor offered a reflection. At the close of the first session in 1979, Jay asked me to be the instructor. I was honored by his request but felt totally inadequate. Doubting I had something worth sharing, and with a now-fluttering stomach, I accepted. After all, St. Mary's was all about challenges. After dinner I sat on a bench by the pond in silence as I'd so often sat in Sidwell's Meeting for Worship. For the past two weeks our small community had lived in an idyllic cocoon removed from the outside world—no TV or radio, only occasional news. During that time America's Skylab I satellite had fallen into the Indian Ocean and President Carter had asked cabinet and senior staff to resign, enabling him to chart a new course. After watching the Sun set over the pond, I rose and calmly walked to the ceremony.

A counselor spoke first connecting passionately with the kids. There was no way to follow. I had no notes. I could only let the counselor's talk carry me like a wave of inspiration. Looking out on our students, I told them what had happened in the world "out there" during our session, a world they'd be returning to the following day. "You'll not return the same person who left two weeks ago," I continued. "You'll take back something of your own that will make the world a better place." In this moment, we all understood this truth. I felt it in my bones. It was that simple. Afterwards staff members greeted me expressing their thanks. I was profoundly glad to be part of this teaching body—teachers of the heart as well as of the head.

REFLECTIONS AND CONTEMPLATIONS

Watch the newsreel of yourself reading this book.

Find one thing that stands out and share it with another person.

Contemplate the following: "You'll take something of your own from this book that will make the world a better place."

Write a story from your life followed by reflection and contemplation questions.

Share it.

NOTES

1 Translated by Asa Cusack. Personal communication, November 2020.
2 An excellent description of the clearness process can be found in Parker Palmer's paper "The Clearness Committee" on the Center for Courage and Renewal's website, accessed October 10, 2020. http://www.couragerenewal.org/clearnesscommittee/
3 HH the Dalai Lama, Archbishop Desmond Tutu, Douglas Abrams (2016). "Joy Meditation—The Eight Pillars" in *The Book of Joy*. New York, Avery, 342–45.
4 Frank Sinatra's classic rendition of Irving Berlin's *Blue Skies* can be found on YouTube, accessed November 2, 2020, https://www.youtube.com/watch?v=ho3eH51rsuM.
5 A detailed description of the game of Jenga can be found on Wikipedia, "Jenga," accessed October 10, 2020, https://en.wikipedia.org/wiki/Jenga.
6 Paley, V.G. (1998). *The Girl with the brown crayon: How children use stories to shape their lives.* Cambridge, Harvard University Press.
7 Adapted from Brady, R. (2003). "Plum Village Tears, Plum Village Joy" in *I Have Arrived, I Am Home: Celebrating Twenty Years of Plum Village* by Thich Nhat Hanh and the Global Plum Village Family. Berkeley: Parallax Press. 190–91.
8 Heifetz, R. (1994). *Leadership without easy answers*. Cambridge: Harvard University Press.
9 Laity, Sister Annabel (2013). "No Coming. No Going" in *Basket of Plums Songbook: Music in the Tradition of Thich Nhat Hanh*, compiled by Joseph Emet. Berkeley: Parallax Press, 20.
10 The recording we played of *Con te partirò* can be found on YouTube, accessed October 10, 2020, https://www.youtube.com/watch?v=Q638RsBSGeA.

POSTSCRIPT

I leave it to a junior high school student who attended St. Mary's to have the final word. Once between sessions, Jay reported to the staff that a counselor had discovered the following note in the drawer of a student bedroom:

Dear Students,

You don't know me, but I slept in the same room as you will be. I'm leaving here today because my two weeks are up. There are a lot of things you will remember about this place, the counselors Karen & Ed, the staff, but most of all the love. If you learn nothing about work and school here, you learn to love and be loved. Well, that's all I have to say, because I'm going to start crying. Keep reminding the staff (especially Karen, Ed, Fred, and Jay) that I love them.

See Ya,
Annie P.

REFLECTIONS AND CONTEMPLATIONS

What have you been grateful for in your experiences as a student? As an educator?

How have you shared your gratitude with others?

RESOURCES

The resources on which I have drawn and which are mentioned in the book began arriving in my life in 1961 when I was sixteen. All are part of who I am today, and, if you've read this book, they have become part of you. Many have been important to me as I walked my path, some recommended by teachers and friends, others showing up seemingly by chance. Not knowing you, it doesn't feel appropriate to make recommendations. As you are ready, I trust that beneficial resources will appear in your life.

Auden, W.H. (1930). *Poems*. London: Faber and Faber.

Bocelli, Andrea and Sarah Brightman (2020). *Con te partirò*. Accessed October 10, 2020. https://www.youtube.com/watch?v=g3ENX3aHlqU.

Brady, Richard (1991). "Present Moment, Wonderful Moment." *The Mindfulness Bell*, no. 5 (Autumn): 30.

———— (2003). "Plum Village Tears, Plum Village Joy." In *I have arrived, I am home: Celebrating twenty years of Plum Village* by Thich Nhat Hanh and the Global Plum Village Family, 190–91. Berkeley: Parallax Press.

———— (2007). "Learning to Stop, Stopping to Learn: Discovering the Contemplative Dimension in Education." *Journal of Transformative Education* 5, no 4: 372–94.

———— (2009). "The Magic Eye: Tuning In During Meeting for Worship." In *Tuning in: Mindfulness in teaching and learning*, edited by Irene McHenry and Richard Brady, 81–2. Philadelphia: Friends Council on Education.

HH the Dalai Lama, Archbishop Desmond Tutu, and Douglas Abrams (2016). *The book of joy*. New York: Avery.

Freire, Paulo (1970). *Pedagogy of the oppressed.* New York: Herder and Herder.

Grubb, Sarah (1794). *Some account of the life and religious labours of Sarah Grubb*, 2nd Edition. London: James Phillips.

Hanh, Thich Nhat (1975). *The miracle of mindfulness: A manual on meditation.* Boston: Beacon Press.

Hanh, Thich Nhat (1987). *Being peace.* Berkeley: Parallax Press.

Hanh, Thich Nhat (1988). *The Sun my heart: From mindfulness to insight contemplation.* Berkeley: Parallax Press.

Hanh, Thich Nhat (1993). *The blooming of a lotus: Guided meditation exercises for healing and transformation.* Boston: Beacon Press.

Hanh, Thich Nhat and Katherine Weare (2017). *Happy teachers change the world.* Berkeley: Parallax Press.

Harrison, Earl (2020). "In Memory of Earl Harrison." *Sidwell Friends School.* Accessed October 18, 2020. https://www.sidwell.edu/retired-former-employees/tributes/~board/news-tributes/post/in-memory-of-earl-harrison.

Heifetz, Ronald (1994). *Leadership without easy answers.* Cambridge: Harvard University Press.

Holt, John (1964). *How children fail.* New York: Pitman.

Jacobs, Harold (1970). *Mathematics, a human endeavor: A textbook for those who think they don't like the subject.* San Francisco: W.H. Freeman.

Kinder, George (1999). *The seven stages of money maturity: Understanding the spirit and value of money in your life.* New York: Dell.

Kirshenbaum, Mira and Charles Foster (1991). *Parent/teen breakthrough: The relationship approach.* New York: Plume.

Kushner, Lawrence (1996). *Invisible lines of connection: Sacred stories of the ordinary.* Woodstock, VT: Jewish Lights.

Laity, Sister Annabel (2013). "No Coming. No Going." In *Basket of plums songbook: music in the tradition of Thich Nhat Hanh*, compiled by Joseph Emet. Berkeley: Parallax Press.

Mailer, Norman (1948). *The naked and the dead.* New York: Rinehart and Company.

McCourt, Frank (2005). *Teacher man: A memoir.* New York: Scribner.

Neill, A.S. (1960). *Summerhill: A radical approach to child rearing.* New York: Hart.

Oliver, Mary (1990). *House of light*. Boston: Beacon Press.

Paley, Vivian Gussin (1998). *The girl with the brown crayon: How children use stories to shape their lives*. Cambridge, Harvard University Press.

Palmer, Parker (1983). *To know as we are known: A spirituality of education*. San Francisco: Harper & Row.

Palmer, Parker (1998). *The courage to teach: Exploring the inner landscape of a teacher's life*. San Francisco: Jossey-Bass.

Palmer, Parker (2020). "The Clearness Committee." *The Center for Courage and Renewal*. Accessed October 10, 2020. http://www.couragerenewal.org/clearnesscommittee/.

Parnes, Sidney J. (1981). *The magic of your mind*. Buffalo: Creative Education Foundation.

Postman, Neil and Charles Weingartner (1969). *Teaching as a subversive activity*. New York: Delta.

Remen, Rachel Naomi (1996). *Kitchen table wisdom: Stories that heal*. New York: Riverhead Books.

Remen, Rachel Naomi (2000). *My grandfather's blessings: Stories of strength, refuge, and belonging*. New York: Riverhead Books.

Rosenberg, Marshall (2015). *Nonviolent communication: A language of life*, 3rd Edition. Encinitas, CA: Puddle Dancer Press.

Rumi, Jelaluddin (1995). *The essential Rumi*. Translated by Coleman Barks with John Moyne, A.J. Arberry, and Reynold Nicholson. San Francisco: Harper.

Salinger, J.D. (1951). *The catcher in the rye*. Boston: Little Brown and Co.

Scattergood, Mary (2009). "Beanie Baby Meditation." In *Tuning in: Mindfulness in teaching and learning*, edited by Irene McHenry and Richard Brady, 33–6. Philadelphia: Friends Council on Education.

Sharan, Yael and Shlomo Sharan (n.d.) "Group Investigation Expands Cooperative Learning." *Educational Leadership* 47, no. 4 (Dec. 89/Jan. 90): 17–21.

Sinatra, Frank (2020). *Blue Skies*. Accessed November 17, 2020. https://www.youtube.com/watch?v=h03eH51rsuM.

Smith, Peggy (2020). "Where Am I." Open Communication. Accessed October 10, 2020. http://www.opencommunication.org/articles/WhichChair-ChoiceFromSelfAwareness.pdf.

Wikipedia (2020a). "Jenga." Accessed October 10. https://en.wikipedia.org/wiki/Jenga.

———— (2020b). "Myers-Briggs Type Indicator." Accessed October 10, 2020. https://en.wikipedia.org/wiki/Myers%E2%80%93Briggs_Type_Indicator.

Wolfe, Thomas (1929). *Look homeward angel: A story of the buried life*. New York: Charles Scribner's Sons.

Zander, Rosamund Stone and Benjamin Zander (2000). *The art of possibility: Transforming professional and personal life*. Boston: Harvard Business School Press.

PERMISSIONS